Virtual Private Networks
Computer Network Security

Contents

Chapter 1

Virtual private network

"VPN" redirects here. For other uses, see VPN (disambiguation).

A **virtual private network** (**VPN**) extends a private network across a public network, such as the Internet. It enables

Internet VPN

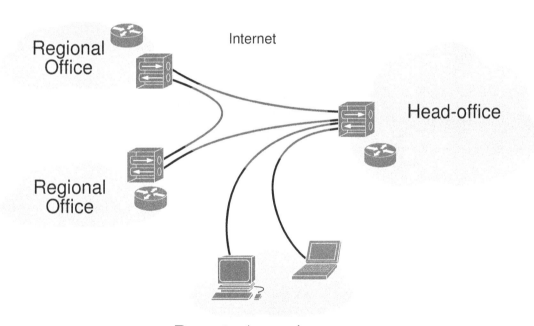

VPN connectivity overview

users to send and receive data across shared or public networks as if their computing devices were directly connected to the private network, and thus are benefiting from the functionality, security and management policies of the private network.[1] A VPN is created by establishing a virtual point-to-point connection through the use of dedicated connections, virtual tunneling protocols, or traffic encryption.

A VPN spanning the Internet is similar to a wide area network (WAN). From a user perspective, the extended network resources are accessed in the same way as resources available within the private network.[2] Traditional VPNs are characterized by a point-to-point topology, and they do not tend to support or connect broadcast domains. Therefore, communication, software, and networking, which are based on OSI layer 2 and broadcast packets, such as NetBIOS used in Windows networking, may not be fully supported or work exactly as they would on a local area network (LAN). VPN variants, such as Virtual Private LAN Service (VPLS), and layer 2 tunneling protocols, are designed to overcome this limitation.

VPNs allow employees to securely access the corporate intranet while traveling outside the office. Similarly, VPNs securely connect geographically separated offices of an organization, creating one cohesive network. VPN technology is also used by individual Internet users to secure their wireless transactions, to circumvent geo-restrictions and censorship, and to connect to proxy servers for the purpose of protecting personal identity and location.

1.1   Types

Early data networks allowed VPN-style remote connectivity through dial-up modems or through leased line connections utilizing Frame Relay and Asynchronous Transfer Mode (ATM) virtual circuits, provisioned through a network owned and operated by telecommunication carriers. These networks are not considered true VPNs because they passively secure the data being transmitted by the creation of logical data streams.[3] They have been replaced by VPNs based on IP and IP/Multiprotocol Label Switching (MPLS) Networks, due to significant cost-reductions and increased bandwidth[4] provided by new technologies such as Digital Subscriber Line (DSL)[5] and fiber-optic networks.

VPNs can be either remote-access (connecting a computer to a network) or site-to-site (connecting two networks). In a corporate setting, remote-access VPNs allow employees to access their company's intranet from home or while traveling outside the office, and site-to-site VPNs allow employees in geographically disparate offices to share one cohesive virtual network. A VPN can also be used to interconnect two similar networks over a dissimilar middle network; for example, two IPv6 networks over an IPv4 network.[6]

VPN systems may be classified by:

- The protocols used to tunnel the traffic

- The tunnel's termination point location, e.g., on the customer edge or network-provider edge

- Whether they offer site-to-site or network-to-network connectivity

- The levels of security provided

- The OSI layer they present to the connecting network, such as Layer 2 circuits or Layer 3 network connectivity

1.2   Security mechanisms

VPNs cannot make online connections completely anonymous, but they can usually increase privacy and security. To prevent disclosure of private information, VPNs typically allow only authenticated remote access using tunneling protocols and encryption techniques.

The VPN security model provides:

- Confidentiality such that even if the network traffic is sniffed at the packet level (see network sniffer and Deep packet inspection), an attacker would only see encrypted data

- Sender authentication to prevent unauthorized users from accessing the VPN

- Message integrity to detect any instances of tampering with transmitted messages

Secure VPN protocols include the following:

- Internet Protocol Security (IPsec) as initially developed by the Internet Engineering Task Force (IETF) for IPv6, which was required in all standards-compliant implementations of IPv6 before RFC 6434 made it only a recommendation.[7] This standards-based security protocol is also widely used with IPv4 and the Layer 2 Tunneling Protocol. Its design meets most security goals: authentication, integrity, and confidentiality. IPsec uses encryption, encapsulating an IP packet inside an IPsec packet. De-encapsulation happens at the end of the tunnel, where the original IP packet is decrypted and forwarded to its intended destination.

- Transport Layer Security (SSL/TLS) can tunnel an entire network's traffic (as it does in the OpenVPN project and SoftEther VPN project[8]) or secure an individual connection. A number of vendors provide remote-access VPN capabilities through SSL. An SSL VPN can connect from locations where IPsec runs into trouble with Network Address Translation and firewall rules.

- Datagram Transport Layer Security (DTLS) - used in Cisco AnyConnect VPN and in OpenConnect VPN[9] to solve the issues SSL/TLS has with tunneling over UDP.

- Microsoft Point-to-Point Encryption (MPPE) works with the Point-to-Point Tunneling Protocol and in several compatible implementations on other platforms.

- Microsoft Secure Socket Tunneling Protocol (SSTP) tunnels Point-to-Point Protocol (PPP) or Layer 2 Tunneling Protocol traffic through an SSL 3.0 channel. (SSTP was introduced in Windows Server 2008 and in Windows Vista Service Pack 1.)

- Multi Path Virtual Private Network (MPVPN). Ragula Systems Development Company owns the registered trademark "MPVPN".[10]

- Secure Shell (SSH) VPN - OpenSSH offers VPN tunneling (distinct from port forwarding) to secure remote connections to a network or to inter-network links. OpenSSH server provides a limited number of concurrent tunnels. The VPN feature itself does not support personal authentication.[11][12][13]

1.2.1 Authentication

Tunnel endpoints must be authenticated before secure VPN tunnels can be established. User-created remote-access VPNs may use passwords, biometrics, two-factor authentication or other cryptographic methods. Network-to-network tunnels often use passwords or digital certificates. They permanently store the key to allow the tunnel to establish automatically, without intervention from the user.

1.3 Routing

Tunneling protocols can operate in a point-to-point network topology that would theoretically not be considered as a VPN, because a VPN by definition is expected to support arbitrary and changing sets of network nodes. But since most router implementations support a software-defined tunnel interface, customer-provisioned VPNs often are simply defined tunnels running conventional routing protocols.

1.3.1 Provider-provisioned VPN building-blocks

Depending on whether a provider-provisioned VPN (PPVPN) operates in layer 2 or layer 3, the building blocks described below may be L2 only, L3 only, or combine them both. Multiprotocol label switching (MPLS) functionality blurs the L2-L3 identity.

RFC 4026 generalized the following terms to cover L2 and L3 VPNs, but they were introduced in RFC 2547.[14] More information on the devices below can also be found in Lewis, Cisco Press.[15]

Customer (C) devices

A device that is within a customer's network and not directly connected to the service provider's network. C devices are not aware of the VPN.

Customer Edge device (CE)

A device at the edge of the customer's network which provides access to the PPVPN. Sometimes it's just a demarcation point between provider and customer responsibility. Other providers allow customers to configure it.

Provider edge device (PE)

A PE is a device, or set of devices, at the edge of the provider network which connects to customer networks through CE devices and presents the provider's view of the customer site. PEs are aware of the VPNs that connect through them, and maintain VPN state.

Provider device (P)

A P device operates inside the provider's core network and does not directly interface to any customer endpoint. It might, for example, provide routing for many provider-operated tunnels that belong to different customers' PPVPNs. While the P device is a key part of implementing PPVPNs, it is not itself VPN-aware and does not maintain VPN state. Its principal role is allowing the service provider to scale its PPVPN offerings, for example, by acting as an aggregation point for multiple PEs. P-to-P connections, in such a role, often are high-capacity optical links between major locations of providers.

1.4   User-visible PPVPN services

This section deals with the types of VPN considered in the IETF.

1.4.1   OSI Layer 2 services

Virtual LAN

A Layer 2 technique that allow for the coexistence of multiple LAN broadcast domains, interconnected via trunks using the IEEE 802.1Q trunking protocol. Other trunking protocols have been used but have become obsolete, including Inter-Switch Link (ISL), IEEE 802.10 (originally a security protocol but a subset was introduced for trunking), and ATM LAN Emulation (LANE).

Virtual private LAN service (VPLS)

Developed by IEEE, VLANs allow multiple tagged LANs to share common trunking. VLANs frequently comprise only customer-owned facilities. Whereas VPLS as described in the above section (OSI Layer 1 services) supports emulation of both point-to-point and point-to-multipoint topologies, the method discussed here extends Layer 2 technologies such as 802.1d and 802.1q LAN trunking to run over transports such as Metro Ethernet.

As used in this context, a VPLS is a Layer 2 PPVPN, rather than a private line, emulating the full functionality of a traditional local area network (LAN). From a user standpoint, a VPLS makes it possible to interconnect several LAN segments over a packet-switched, or optical, provider core; a core transparent to the user, making the remote LAN segments behave as one single LAN.[16]

In a VPLS, the provider network emulates a learning bridge, which optionally may include VLAN service.

Pseudo wire (PW)

PW is similar to VPLS, but it can provide different L2 protocols at both ends. Typically, its interface is a WAN protocol such as Asynchronous Transfer Mode or Frame Relay. In contrast, when aiming to provide the appearance of a LAN contiguous between two or more locations, the Virtual Private LAN service or IPLS would be appropriate.

Ethernet over IP tunneling

EtherIP (RFC 3378) is an Ethernet over IP tunneling protocol specification. EtherIP has only packet encapsulation mechanism. It has no confidentiality nor message integrity protection. EtherIP was introduced in the FreeBSD network stack [17] and the SoftEther VPN[18] server program.

IP-only LAN-like service (IPLS)

A subset of VPLS, the CE devices must have L3 capabilities; the IPLS presents packets rather than frames. It may support IPv4 or IPv6.

1.4.2   OSI Layer 3 PPVPN architectures

This section discusses the main architectures for PPVPNs, one where the PE disambiguates duplicate addresses in a single routing instance, and the other, virtual router, in which the PE contains a virtual router instance per VPN. The former approach, and its variants, have gained the most attention.

One of the challenges of PPVPNs involves different customers using the same address space, especially the IPv4 private address space.[19] The provider must be able to disambiguate overlapping addresses in the multiple customers' PPVPNs.

BGP/MPLS PPVPN

In the method defined by RFC 2547, BGP extensions advertise routes in the IPv4 VPN address family, which are of the form of 12-byte strings, beginning with an 8-byte Route Distinguisher (RD) and ending with a 4-byte IPv4 address. RDs disambiguate otherwise duplicate addresses in the same PE.

PEs understand the topology of each VPN, which are interconnected with MPLS tunnels, either directly or via P routers. In MPLS terminology, the P routers are Label Switch Routers without awareness of VPNs.

Virtual router PPVPN

The Virtual Router architecture,[20][21] as opposed to BGP/MPLS techniques, requires no modification to existing routing protocols such as BGP. By the provisioning of logically independent routing domains, the customer operating a VPN is completely responsible for the address space. In the various MPLS tunnels, the different PPVPNs are disambiguated by their label, but do not need routing distinguishers.

1.4.3   Unencrypted tunnels

Main article: Tunneling protocol

Some virtual networks may not use encryption to protect the privacy of data. While VPNs often provide security, an unencrypted overlay network does not neatly fit within the secure or trusted categorization. For example, a tunnel set up between two hosts that used Generic Routing Encapsulation (GRE) would in fact be a virtual private network, but neither secure nor trusted.

Native plaintext tunneling protocols include Layer 2 Tunneling Protocol (L2TP) when it is set up without IPsec and Point-to-Point Tunneling Protocol (PPTP) or Microsoft Point-to-Point Encryption (MPPE).

1.5   Trusted delivery networks

Trusted VPNs do not use cryptographic tunneling, and instead rely on the security of a single provider's network to protect the traffic.[22]

- Multi-Protocol Label Switching (MPLS) often overlays VPNs, often with quality-of-service control over a trusted delivery network.

- Layer 2 Tunneling Protocol (L2TP)[23] which is a standards-based replacement, and a compromise taking the good features from each, for two proprietary VPN protocols: Cisco's Layer 2 Forwarding (L2F)[24] (obsolete as of 2009) and Microsoft's Point-to-Point Tunneling Protocol (PPTP).[25]

From the security standpoint, VPNs either trust the underlying delivery network, or must enforce security with mechanisms in the VPN itself. Unless the trusted delivery network runs among physically secure sites only, both trusted and secure models need an authentication mechanism for users to gain access to the VPN.

1.6   VPNs in mobile environments

Mobile virtual private networks are used in settings where an endpoint of the VPN is not fixed to a single IP address, but instead roams across various networks such as data networks from cellular carriers or between multiple Wi-Fi access points.[26] Mobile VPNs have been widely used in public safety, where they give law enforcement officers access to mission-critical applications, such as computer-assisted dispatch and criminal databases, while they travel between different subnets of a mobile network.[27] They are also used in field service management and by healthcare organizations,[28] among other industries.

Increasingly, mobile VPNs are being adopted by mobile professionals who need reliable connections.[28] They are used for roaming seamlessly across networks and in and out of wireless coverage areas without losing application sessions or dropping the secure VPN session. A conventional VPN can live such events because the network tunnel is disrupted, causing applications to disconnect, time out,[26] or fail, or even cause the computing device itself to crash.[28]

Instead of logically tying the endpoint of the network tunnel to the physical IP address, each tunnel is bound to a permanently associated IP address at the device. The mobile VPN software handles the necessary network authentication and maintains the network sessions in a manner transparent to the application and the user.[26] The Host Identity Protocol (HIP), under study by the Internet Engineering Task Force, is designed to support mobility of hosts by separating the role of IP addresses for host identification from their locator functionality in an IP network. With HIP a mobile host maintains its logical connections established via the host identity identifier while associating with different IP addresses when roaming between access networks.

1.7   VPN on routers

With the increasing use of VPNs, many have started deploying VPN connectivity on routers for additional security and encryption of data transmission by using various cryptographic techniques.[29] Setting up VPN services on a router allows any connected device to use the VPN network while it is enabled. This also creates VPN services on devices that do not have native VPN clients such as smart-TVs, gaming consoles etc.

Many router manufacturers, such as Cisco, Linksys, Asus, and Netgear supply their routers with built-in VPN clients.

Since these routers do not support all the major VPN protocols, such as OpenVPN.

Limitations: Not every router compatible with open source firmware which depends on the built-in flash memory and processor. Firmwares like DD-WRT require a minimum of 2 MiB flash memory and Broadcom chipsets. Setting up VPN services on a router requires a deeper knowledge of network security and careful installation. Minor misconfiguration of VPN connections can leave the network vulnerable. Performance will vary depending on the ISP and their reliability.[30]

1.8 Networking limitations

One major limitation of traditional VPNs is that they are point-to-point, and do not tend to support or connect broadcast domains. Therefore, communication, software, and networking, which are based on layer 2 and broadcast packets, such as NetBIOS used in Windows networking, may not be fully supported or work exactly as they would on a real LAN. Variants on VPN, such as Virtual Private LAN Service (VPLS), and layer 2 tunneling protocols, are designed to overcome this limitation.

1.9 See also

- Anonymizer
- Geo-Blocking
- Internet Privacy
- Opportunistic encryption
- Split tunneling
- Mediated VPN
- VPNBook
- UT-VPN
- Tinc (protocol)
- DMVPN (Dynamic Multipoint VPN)
- Virtual Private LAN Service

1.10 References

[1] Mason, Andrew G. (2002). *Cisco Secure Virtual Private Network*. Cisco Press. p. 7.

[2] Microsoft Technet. "Virtual Private Networking: An Overview".

[3] Cisco Systems, et al. *Internet working Technologies Handbook, Third Edition*. Cisco Press, 2000, p. 232.

[4] Lewis, Mark. *Comparing, Designing. And Deploying VPNs*. Cisco Press, 2006, p. 5

[5] International Engineering Consortium. *Digital Subscriber Line 2001*. Intl. Engineering Consortium, 2001, p. 40.

[6] Technet Lab. "IPv6 traffic over VPN connections".

[7] RFC 6434, "IPv6 Node Requirements", E. Jankiewicz, J. Loughney, T. Narten (December 2011)

[8] SoftEther VPN: Using HTTPS Protocol to Establish VPN Tunnels

[9] "OpenConnect". Retrieved 2013-04-08. OpenConnect is a client for Cisco's AnyConnect SSL VPN [...] OpenConnect is not officially supported by, or associated in any way with, Cisco Systems. It just happens to interoperate with their equipment.

[10] Trademark Applications and Registrations Retrieval (TARR)

[11] OpenBSD ssh manual page, VPN section

[12] Unix Toolbox section on SSH VPN

[13] Ubuntu SSH VPN how-to

[14] E. Rosen & Y. Rekhter (March 1999). "RFC 2547 BGP/MPLS VPNs". Internet Engineering Task Force (IETF).

[15] Lewis, Mark (2006). *Comparing, designing, and deploying VPNs* (1st print. ed.). Indianapolis, Ind.: Cisco Press. pp. 5–6. ISBN 1587051796.

[16] *Ethernet Bridging (OpenVPN)*

[17] Glyn M Burton: RFC 3378 EtherIP with FreeBSD, 03 February 2011

[18] net-security.org news: Multi-protocol SoftEther VPN becomes open source, January 2014

[19] Address Allocation for Private Internets, RFC 1918, Y. Rekhter *et al.*, February 1996

[20] RFC 2917, *A Core MPLS IP VPN Architecture*

[21] RFC 2918, E. Chen (September 2000)

[22] Cisco Systems, Inc. (2004). *Internetworking Technologies Handbook*. Networking Technology Series (4 ed.). Cisco Press. p. 233. ISBN 9781587051197. Retrieved 2013-02-15. [...] VPNs using dedicated circuits, such as Frame Relay [...] are sometimes called *trusted VPN*s, because customers trust that the network facilities operated by the service providers will not be compromised.

[23] Layer Two Tunneling Protocol "L2TP", RFC 2661, W. Townsley *et al.*, August 1999

[24] IP Based Virtual Private Networks, RFC 2341, A. Valencia *et al.*, May 1998

[25] Point-to-Point Tunneling Protocol (PPTP), RFC 2637, K. Hamzeh *et al.*, July 1999

[26] Phifer, Lisa. "Mobile VPN: Closing the Gap", *SearchMobileComputing.com*, July 16, 2006.

[27] Willett, Andy. "Solving the Computing Challenges of Mobile Officers", *www.officer.com*, May, 2006.

[28] Cheng, Roger. "Lost Connections", *The Wall Street Journal*, December 11, 2007.

[29] "Encryption and Security Protocols in a VPN". Retrieved 2015-09-23.

[30] 31West - Nancy Pais. "VPN on Routers: Introduction".

1.11   Further reading

- Kelly, Sean (August 2001). "Necessity is the mother of VPN invention". *Communication News*: 26–28. ISSN 0010-3632. Archived from the original on 2001-12-17.

Chapter 2

AceVPN

AceVPN or **Ace VPN** is a U.S.-based Virtual private network (VPN) subscription provider. It offers private network services over a public network.[1][2]

A VPN established a virtual point-to-point connection through dedicated connections, tunneling protocols, and virtual traffic encryption. VPNs enable users to maintain privacy while browsing public networks.[3] Ace has been used to circumvent IP restrictions in certain areas to access internet and app functions.[2]

Beginning in May of 2013, Ace VPN usage soared when the Turkish government shut down Facebook and Twitter access within its borders in retaliation of the Gezi Park protests. The crackdown on internet usage was seen as a major human rights violation and VPNs became popular in the nation and elsewhere.[4] Ace VPN has remained one of the most popular VPNs in Turkey as the nation's Parliament has begun debating the controversial topic of internet censorship.[5][6]

Ace VPN was featured at DEF CON, an annual hacker convention, as a means of avoiding hackers tracking Internet search histories.[1]

Ace VPN currently holds an active Warrant canary.[7]

2.1 References

[1] Sutter, John (Aug 6, 2011). "DEF CON: The event that scares hackers". *CNN*.

[2] "Apps without borders: how to access US-only audio and video apps on your iPhone". *APC Mag*. Feb 1, 2011.

[3] Mason, Andrew G. (2002). *Cisco Secure Virtual Private Network*. Cisco Press. p. 7.

[4] Butcher, Mike (Jun 1, 2013). "As Anti-Government Protests Erupt In Istanbul, Facebook And Twitter Appear Suddenly Throttled". *Tech Crunch*.

[5] "http://www.demokrathaber.net/internet-dunyasi/internet-yasaklari-nasil-delinebilir-h28163.html". *Demokrat Haber*.

[6] "Youtube dns ayarları 2014 nasıl değiştirilir ve yöntemleri güncek key". *Kirikhan*.

[7] "Canary List". Canarywatch. Retrieved 21 June 2015.

Chapter 3

AnchorFree

AnchorFree is a software company that provides a virtual private network (VPN) for secure web browsing.[1] The company is led by David Gorodyansky, who founded the firm in 2005 together with his friend Eugene Malobrodksy.[1][2][3] The company is headquartered in Mountain View, California.[1]

3.1 Platforms and users

The company works with a "freemium" model, providing free software with advertisements, and a paid version without ads.[4] The software is available for desktops, smart phones and tablet computers using Microsoft Windows, Mac OS X, Android and iOS operating systems.[4][4][5] The software has been downloaded 120 million times and has 20 million active monthly users in 190 countries.[2][6]

Hotspot Shield has been used in countries where the Internet is censored because the software allows users to gain access to websites privately and thus remain uncensored.[7][8] AnchorFree has data centers in the United States, Japan, Germany and Switzerland, locations which are only partly subject to Internet censorship.[7] The firm reported an increase in its Egyptian user base from 100,000 users to one million during the Arab Spring.[7][9] During this time, the program was used to access social media websites like Twitter to organize protests.[7][9] The firm's website is now blocked from some Middle Eastern countries, China and Thailand; the company set up an auto-reply email with a VPN software attachment to circumvent the censorship and provide clients with the application.[7] It was also used in Tunisia and Libya before the Arab Spring.[8]

In 2012, after reaching 60 million downloads, the company announced it had raised $52 million of financing from Goldman Sachs.[10]

3.2 Reviews and awards

A March 2012 review on CNET's web site complained about visual clutter.[11] Seth Rosenblatt credited the program with improvements in its design and installation but urged the company to serve its ads in a less annoying way. Rosenblatt still described it as a must-have utility for anybody who uses public Wi-Fi networks.[12]

In an April 2012 review, *PC Magazine* called Hotspot Shield "a useful tool to have if you spend a lot of time on public Wi-Fi networks".[13] The reviewer, Fahmida Rashid, had concerns about the program automatically inserting an ad for the Hotspot Shield service into whatever web page the user was visiting. She also noted that the free version of Hotspot Shield was receiving a tracking pixel and that the address of the site the ad was being displayed on was being sent back to rpt.anchorfree.com. She commented on the ads: "*The free version of Hotspot Shield's ad-delivery mechanism and how it affects Web browsers tempered my enthusiasm for the service a bit... The ads make the experience just annoying enough that users are willing to upgrade to Elite.*" She did see the logic of using ads to make the paid version more appealing. *PC Magazine* marked the program as an Editor's Choice.[13]

The Appy Awards named Hotspot Shield the best Online Security/Privacy Application in 2013.[14]

Forbes magazine, for which the company's CEO has written articles,[15] named AnchorFree America's sixth most promising company in 2013.[16][17]

Business Insider named AnchorFree as one of the 15 most important security startups of 2013.[18]

3.3 References

[1] "AnchorFree". *CrunchBase*. Retrieved 8 April 2013.

[2] Konrad, Alex. "AnchorFree: A road warrior's friend, a censor's foe". *CNN Money*. Retrieved 8 April 2013.

[3] Empson, Rip. "With its Hotspot Shield hitting 60M Downloads, AnchorFree Lands a Whopping $52M from Goldman Sachs". *TechCrunch*. Retrieved 8 April 2013.

[4] Velazco, Chris. "AnchorFree brings their Hotspot Shield mobile security app to Android". *TechCrunch*. Retrieved 8 April 2013.

[5] Messeih, Nancy. "Hotspot Shield: A quiet hero for Internet privacy and security around the world". *TNW*. Retrieved 8 April 2013.

[6] Wauters, Robin. "AnchorFree CEO tells us why 100 million people downloaded Hotspot Shield to date (video)". *TNW*. Retrieved 8 April 2013.

[7] Colao, J.J. "How To Thwart Hackers And Dictators With One Free Download". Forbes. Retrieved 8 April 2013.

[8] Messieh, Nancy. "Hotspot Shield: A quiet hero for Internet privacy and security around the world". *TNW*. Retrieved 8 April 2013.

[9] Markowitz, Eric. "David Gorodyansky and Eugene Malobrodsky, Founders of AnchorFree". *Inc*. Retrieved 8 April 2013.

[10] Empson, Rip (2012-05-21). "With Its Hotspot Shield Hitting 60M Downloads, AnchorFree Lands A Whopping $52M From Goldman Sachs". Tech Crunch. Retrieved 2014-05-07.

[11] Rosenblatt, Seth (March 15, 2012). "HotSpot Shield's new shine not without blemish". *CNet Download Blog*.

[12] Rosenblatt, Seth (March 14, 2012). "HotSpot Shield". *download.cnet.com*.

[13] Rashid, Fahmida (April 13, 2012). "Hotspot Shield Elite". *PC Magazine*.

[14] "Appy Awards 2013". *MediaPost*. Retrieved 8 April 2013.

[15] "David Gorodyansky". Forbes. May 28, 2014. Retrieved 14 June 2014.

[16] "Forbes names AnchorFree as America's Sixth Most Promising Company". *MarketWire*. Retrieved 8 April 2013.

[17] Colao, JJ; Canal, Emily. "America's Most Promising Companies". Forbes. Retrieved 8 April 2013.

[18] Bort, Julie. "The 15 most important security startups of 2013". *Business Insider*. Retrieved 8 April 2013.

3.4 External links

- Official website
- Hotspot Shield Official Website

Chapter 4

Avast! SecureLine VPN

The **Avast! SecureLine VPN** (stylised **avast! SecureLine VPN** or just **SecureLine VPN**) is a subscription based Virtual Private Network (VPN) developed by Avast Software. It is available on Android, Microsoft Windows, Mac OS X and iOS[1] The premise of the software is to secure connection to public Wi-Fi systems to stop hackers getting into the user's computer.[2] Similar to other VPN's, SecureLine works by making the user appear in a different place via changing the users IP address, this can bypass internet censorship for the country the user is in or Wi-Fi the user is using.[3] The VPN automatically enables when the user connects to a public Wi-Fi.[4]

SecureLine can only be used by users of Avast! Anti-Virus.[4]

4.1 References

[1] "Avast SecureLine VPN - Secure any public Wi-Fi". Avast Software. Retrieved 19 June 2015.

[2] Zorz, Mirko (19 May 2014). "Secure public WiFi with avast! SecureLine for iOS". Net-security.org. Retrieved 19 June 2015.

[3] "Avast SecureLine VPN". *Download.com*. Retrieved 19 June 2015.

[4] Rashid, Fahmida (25 June 2015). "avast! SecureLine Review & Rating". PC Mag. Retrieved 19 June 2015.

Chapter 5

BTGuard

BTGuard is a Virtual Private Network service specifically designed for anonymous filesharing through the BitTorrent network operated in Canada. Established in 2008, the service legally reroutes a customer's internet traffic through a different IP address.[1]

It has received attention and positive reviews by websites such as TorrentFreak.com, and offers both a traditional VPN as well as versions of common BitTorrent clients such as uTorrent that have been specifically modified to transfer files anonymously through their anonymous proxy.[2]

5.1 See also

- VPN

- Proxy Server

5.2 References

[1] Stone, Jeff (18 February 2013). "BT Guard Review: VPN's Frequent Downtime, Poor Customer Service Vs. Affordability, Convenience". *International Business Times*. Retrieved 21 November 2014.

[2] Article on TorrentFreak.com: "BTGuard Review: How Does it Work?" http://torrentfreak.com/make-bittorrent-transfers-anonymous-with-btguard

5.3 External links

- BTGuard Official Website

Chapter 6

CAPRI OS

CAPRI OS is a National Security Agency codename for a project that is sent SSH and SSL intercepts for post-processing.[1]

6.1 References

[1] "Intro to the VPN Exploitation Process" (PDF). *http://www.spiegel.de/*. Spiegel.

Chapter 7

Darknet

This article is about networking technology. For other uses, see Darknet (disambiguation). For websites that exist on top of this technology, see Dark Web.

A **darknet** (or **dark net**) is an overlay network that can only be accessed with specific software, configurations, or authorization, often using non-standard communications protocols and ports. Two typical darknet types are friend-to-friend[1] networks (usually used for file sharing with a peer-to-peer connection)[2] and anonymity networks such as Tor via an anonymized series of connections.

The reciprocal term for an encrypted darknet is clearnet[3][4][5] or surface web when referring to search engine indexable content.[6]

7.1 Origins

Originally coined in the 1970s to designate networks which were isolated from ARPANET (which evolved into the Internet) for security purposes,[7] darknets were able to receive data from ARPANET but had addresses which did not appear in the network lists and would not answer pings or other inquiries.

The term gained public acceptance following publication of "The Darknet and the Future of Content Distribution",[8] a 2002 paper by Peter Biddle, Paul England, Marcus Peinado, and Bryan Willman, four employees of Microsoft who argued that the presence of the darknet was the primary hindrance to the development of workable DRM technologies and inevitability of copyright infringement.

7.1.1 Sub-cultures

Journalist J. D. Lasica in his 2005 book *Darknet: Hollywood's War Against the Digital Generation* describes the darknet's reach encompassing file sharing networks.[9] Consequently, in 2014, journalist Jamie Bartlett in his book *The Dark Net* would use it as a term to describe a range of underground and emergent sub cultures, including

- Social media racists

- Camgirls

- Self Harm communities

- Darknet drug markets

- Cryptoanarchists

- Transhumanists.[10]

As of 2015, "The Darknet" is often used interchangeably with "The Dark Web" due to the quantity of hidden services on Tor's darknet. The term is often used inaccurately and interchangeably with the Deep Web search due to Tor's history as a platform that could not be search indexed. Mixing uses of both of these terms has been described as inaccurate,[11] with some commentators recommending the terms be used in distinct fashions.[12][13]

7.2 Uses

Darknets in general may be used for various reasons, such as:

- To better protect the privacy rights of citizens from targeted and mass surveillance
- Protecting dissidents from political reprisal; see Arab Spring
- Whistleblowing and news leaks
- Computer crime (hacking, file corruption etc)
- Sale of restricted goods on darknet markets
- File sharing (pornography, confidential files, illegal or counterfeit software etc.)

7.3 Software

All darknets require specific software installed or network configurations made to access them, such as Tor which can be accessed via a customised browser from Vidalia, aka the Tor browser bundle or alternatively via a proxy server configured to perform the same function.

Main page: Category:Anonymity networks

7.3.1 Active

- Tor (The onion router) is an anonymity network that also features a darknet - its "hidden services". It is the most popular instance of a darknet.[14]
- I2P (Invisible Internet Project) is another overlay network that features a darknet whose sites are called "Eepsites".
- Freenet is a popular darknet (friend-to-friend) by default; since version 0.7 it can run as a "opennet" (peer nodes are discovered automatically).
- RetroShare can be run as a darknet (friend-to-friend) by default to perform anonymous file transfers if DHT and Discovery features are disabled.
- GNUnet is a darknet if the "F2F (network) topology" option is enabled.
- Zeronet is open source software aimed to build an internet-like computer network of peer-to-peer users of Tor.
- Syndie is software used to publish distributed forums over the anonymous networks of I2P, Tor and Freenet.
- OneSwarm can be run as a darknet for friend-to-friend file-sharing.
- Tribler can be run as a darknet for file-sharing.

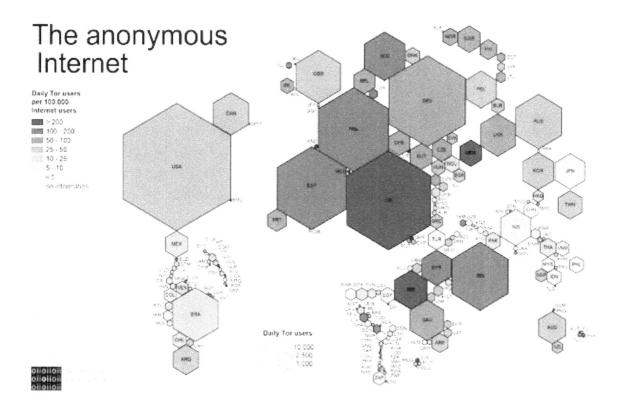

A cartogram illustrating Tor usage

7.3.2 Defunct

- AllPeers
- anoNet
- Turtle F2F
- WASTE

7.4 See also

- Crypto-anarchism
- Private P2P
- Sneakernet
- Internet privacy
- Virtual private network (VPN)

7.5 References

[1] Wood, Jessica (2010). "The Darknet: A Digital Copyright Revolution" (PDF). *Richmond Journal of Law and Technology* **16** (4): 15–17. Retrieved 25 October 2011.

[2] Mansfield-Devine, Steve (December 2009). "Darknets". *Computer Fraud & Security* **2009** (12): 4–6. doi:10.1016/S1361-3723(09)70150-2.

[3] Miller, Tessa (10 January 2014). "How Can I Stay Anonymous with Tor?". *Life Hacker*. Retrieved 7 June 2015.

[4] Torpey, Kyle (2 December 2014). "Blockchain.info Launches Tor Hidden Service". *Inside Bitcoins*. Retrieved 9 June 2015.

[5] Roger, Jolly. "Clearnet vs Hidden Services—Why You Should Be Careful". *Jolly Roger's Security Guide for Beginners*. DeepDotWeb. Retrieved 4 June 2015.

[6] Barratt, Monica (15 January 2015). "A Discussion About Dark Net Terminology". *Drugs, Internet, Society*. Retrieved 14 June 2015.

[7] "Om Darknet". Archived from the original on 25 March 2015. Retrieved 11 March 2012.

[8] Biddle, Peter; England, Paul; Peinado, Marcus; Willman, Bryan (18 November 2002). *The Darknet and the Future of Content Distribution* (PDF). ACM Workshop on Digital Rights Management. Washington, D.C.: Microsoft Corporation. Retrieved 10 October 2012.

[9] Lasica, J. D. (2005). *Darknets: Hollywood's War Against the Digital Generation*. Hoboken, NJ: J. Wiley & Sons. ISBN 0-471-68334-5.

[10] Ian, Burrell (28 August 2014). "The Dark Net:Inside the Digital Underworld by Jamie Bartlett, book review". Retrieved 3 June 2015.

[11] "Clearing Up Confusion – Deep Web vs. Dark Web". *BrightPlanet*.

[12] NPR Staff (25 May 2014). "Going Dark: The Internet Behind The Internet". Retrieved 29 May 2015.

[13] Greenberg, Andy (19 November 2014). "Hacker Lexicon: What Is the Dark Web?". Retrieved 6 June 2015.

[14] "Anticounterfeiting on the Dark Web - Distinctions between the Surface Web, Dark Web and Deep Web" (PDF). 13 April 2015. Retrieved 1 June 2015.

7.6 External links

- Boutin, Paul (January 28, 2004). "See You on the Darknet". *Slate*.

- "File-sharing 'darknet' unveiled". *BBC News*. August 16, 2006.

- Darknet 101 - introduction for non technical people

Chapter 8

Decentralized network 42

Decentralized network 42 (also known as **dn42**) is a decentralized peer-to-peer network built using VPNs and software/hardware BGP routers.

While other darknets try to establish anonymity for their participants, that is not what dn42 aims for. It is a network to explore routing technologies used in the Internet and tries to establish direct non-NAT-ed connections between the members.

The network is not fully meshed. Dn42 hardly uses physical links between the single networks but virtual ones. These virtual links use the Internet as transport but are logically independent from it, you can treat a virtual link more or less like a fiber or copper line.[1] Everybody has a VPN connection to one or more participants.[2] The connections are bound to a public IP address. If you decide to use GRE or SIT the diactc (Diac24 Tunnel Controller) updates the public IP address of the connection endpoint on IP changes. OpenVPN is capable of doing this without external help. Over the VPN connection BGP is used for inter AS routing and by default OSPF for intra AS routing, but participants may obviously use any protocol they see fit for the purposes of routing inside of their own AS.

8.1 Technical setup

8.1.1 Address space

Network address space for IPv4 consists of private subnets: 172.22.0.0/15 is the main subnet.[3] Note that other private address ranges may also be announced in dn42, as the network is interconnected with other similar projects. Most notably, ChaosVPN uses 172.31.0.0/16 and parts of 10.0.0.0/8.[4]

For IPv6, both Unique Local Address (ULA, the IPv6 equivalent of private address range) and Globally routable addresses are used, with a preference for ULA.[3]

8.1.2 AS numbers

In order to use BGP, even in a private environment, Autonomous System Numbers are needed. dn42 uses several private or reserved AS numbers ranges, including 64512 to 64855 and 76100 to 76199.[5] In June 2014, dn42 started using a new private range, 4242420000 to 4242429999,[6] part of larger private range defined by RFC 6996.

8.1.3 BGP routers

Hardware used on dn42 consists of routers, which aren't always a cheap solution. There are mainly four implementations for BGP on default hardware. The most common in dn42 is Quagga, a fork of the no longer maintained GNU Zebra, which runs on most Unices from Linux over *BSD to OpenSolaris. Also used in dn42 is OpenBGPD which runs on

OpenBSD. There are also the "enterprise class" XORP and the simplistic BIRD, however those are not very common in dn42. There were also some machines running JunOS, the Juniper Operating system, which is used with professional routing hardware.[1]

8.2   References

[1] "Technical details of dn42". 2009-09-19. Retrieved 6 June 2010.

[2] "Real-time dn42 network map". Retrieved 27 Oct 2013.

[3] "dn42 address space". Retrieved 9 June 2014.

[4] "ChaosVPN IP ranges". Retrieved 9 June 2014.

[5] "Frequently Asked Questions". Retrieved 9 June 2014.

[6] "AS numbers". Retrieved 9 June 2014.

8.3   External links

- Official website

Chapter 9

DirectAccess

DirectAccess, also known as Unified Remote Access, is a VPN-like technology that provides intranet connectivity to client computers when they are connected to the Internet. Unlike many traditional VPN connections, which must be initiated and terminated by explicit user action, DirectAccess connections are designed to connect automatically as soon as the computer connects to the Internet. DirectAccess was introduced in Windows Server 2008 R2, providing this service to Windows 7 and Windows 8 "Enterprise" edition clients. In 2010, Microsoft Forefront Unified Access Gateway (UAG) was released, which simplifies[1][2] the deployment of DirectAccess for Windows 2008 R2, and includes additional components that make it easier to integrate without the need to deploy IPv6 on the network, and with a dedicated user interface for the configuration and monitoring. Some requirements and limitations that were part of the design of DirectAccess with Windows Server 2008 R2 and UAG have been changed (see requirements below). While DirectAccess is based on Microsoft technology, third-party solutions exist for accessing internal UNIX and Linux servers through DirectAccess.[3] With Windows Server 2012, DirectAccess is fully integrated[4] into the operating system, providing a user interface to configure and native IPv6 and IPv4 support.

9.1   Technology

DirectAccess establishes IPsec tunnels from the client to the DirectAccess server, and uses IPv6 to reach intranet resources or other DirectAccess clients. This technology encapsulates the IPv6 traffic over IPv4 to be able to reach the intranet over the Internet, which still (mostly) relies on IPv4 traffic. All traffic to the intranet is encrypted using IPsec and encapsulated in IPv4 packets, which means that in most cases, no configuration of firewalls or proxies should be required.[5] A DirectAccess client can use one of several tunneling technologies, depending on the configuration of the network the client is connected to. The client can use 6to4, Teredo tunneling, or IP-HTTPS, provided the server is configured correctly to be able to use them. For example, a client that is connected to the Internet directly will use 6to4, but if it is inside a NATed network, it will use Teredo instead. In addition, Windows Server 2012 provides two backward compatibility services DNS64 and NAT64, which allows DirectAccess clients to communicate with servers inside the corporate network even if those servers are only capable of IPv4 networking. Due to the globally routable nature of IPv6, computers on the corporate network can also initiate a connection to DirectAccess clients, which allows them to remotely manage (Manage Out) these clients at any time.[6]

9.2   Requirements

DirectAccess With Windows Server 2008 R2 or UAG requires:

- One or more DirectAccess servers running Windows Server 2008 R2 with two network adapters: one that is connected directly to the Internet, and a second that is connected to the intranet.

- On the DirectAccess server, at least two consecutive, public IPv4 addresses assigned to the network adapter that is connected to the Internet.

- DirectAccess clients running Windows 7 "Ultimate" or "Enterprise" editions or Windows 8 "Enterprise" edition clients

- At least one domain controller and Domain Name System (DNS) server running Windows Server 2008 SP2 or Windows Server 2008 R2.

- Public key infrastructure (PKI) to issue computer certificates.

DirectAccess With Windows Server 2012 requires:

- One or more DirectAccess servers running Windows Server 2012 with one or more network adapters.

- At least one domain controller and Domain Name System (DNS) server running Windows Server 2008 SP2 or Windows Server 2008 R2.

- DirectAccess clients running Windows 7 "Ultimate" or "Enterprise" editions or Windows 8 "Enterprise" edition clients

- A Public Key Infrastructure is not required for Windows 8 Clients. [7]

Smart card certificates, and health certificates for Network Access Protection may be used along with PKI.

9.3   Problems

There are problems in the functionality of DirectAccess in Windows Server 2008 R2 . These are listed as follows:

- Windows 2008 R2 version of DirectAccess (not UAG version) forces you to use IPv6 end to end. This was due to Microsoft not including the NAT64 (IPv6 to IPv4) component in the basic version of DirectAccess included in Windows 2008 R2. NAT64 was included with Microsoft Unified Access Gateway (UAG) allowing IPv6 to IPv4 connectivity. Windows Server 2012 versions of DirectAccess have rectified this issue and are fully IPv4 supported.

9.4   References

[1] Microsoft Forefront Unified Access Gateway 2010

[2] Windows Server Division WebLog

[3] Centrify DirectSecure - Integrating Windows DirectAccess with UNIX and Linux Systems

[4] What's New in DirectAccess in Windows Server

[5] DirectAccess: Microsoft's Newest VPN Solution - Part 1: Overview of Current Remote Access Solutions

[6] Ben-Ari, Erez (2012). *Windows Server 2012 Unified Remote Access Planning and Deployment*. London: Packt. p. 189. ISBN 1849688281. Retrieved 27 December 2012.

[7] What's New in DirectAccess in Windows Server

9.5 External links

- Microsoft's DirectAccess in Windows Server 2012

- Microsoft's DirectAccess in Windows Server 2008 R2

- MS-IPHTTPS on MSDN: includes PDF with specification.

- Blogger's posting on DirectAccess

- Richard Hicks' DirectAccess Blog

- Differences between UAG and native 2008 R2 DirectAccess

Chapter 10

Dynamic Multipoint Virtual Private Network

Dynamic Multipoint Virtual Private Network (DMVPN)[1] is a dynamic tunneling form of a virtual private network (VPN) supported on Cisco IOS-based routers, Huawei AR G3 routers[2] and USG firewalls, and on Unix-like operating systems.

10.1 Benefits

DMVPN provides the capability for creating a dynamic-mesh VPN network without having to pre-configure (static) all possible tunnel end-point peers, including IPsec (Internet Protocol Security) and ISAKMP (Internet Security Association and Key Management Protocol) peers. DMVPN is initially configured to build out a hub-and-spoke network by statically configuring the hubs (VPN headends) on the spokes, no change in the configuration on the hub is required to accept new spokes. Using this initial hub-and-spoke network, tunnels between spokes can be dynamically built on demand (dynamic-mesh) without additional configuration on the hubs or spokes. This dynamic-mesh capability alleviates the need for any load on the hub to route data between the spoke networks.

10.2 Technologies

- Generic Routing Encapsulation (GRE), RFC 1701, or multipoint GRE if spoke-to-spoke tunnels are desired

- NHRP (next-hop resolution protocol), RFC 2332

- IPsec (Internet Protocol Security) using an IPsec profile, which is associated to a virtual tunnel interface in IOS software. All traffic sent via the tunnel is encrypted per the policy configured (IPsec transform set)

- An IP based routing protocol, EIGRP, OSPF, RIPv2, BGP or ODR (DMVPN hub-and-spoke only).[3]

10.2.1 Internal routing

Routing protocols such as OSPF, EIGRPv1 or v2 or BGP are generally run between the hub and spoke to allow for growth and scalability. The Cisco-proprietary EIGRP is generally considered preferable as it is an advanced distance vector style protocol which better matches with the NBMA (Non-Broadcast Multi-Access) style network that DMVPN builds. Both EIGRP and BGP allow a higher number of supported spokes per hub.[4]

10.2.2 Encryption

As with GRE tunnels, DMVPN allows for several encryption schemes (including none) for the encryption of data traversing the tunnels. For security reasons Cisco recommend that customers use AES.[5]

10.3 References

[1] Dynamic Multipoint IPsec VPNs (Using Multipoint GRE/NHRP to Scale IPsec VPNs)

[2] Huawei DSVPN Configuration

[3] DMVPN Design Guide: Using a Routing Protocol Across the VPN

[4] DMVPN Design Guide: Routing Protocol Configuration

[5] DMVPN Design Guide: Best Practices and Known Limitations

10.4 External links

- Cisco Systems

- DMVPN Overview

- Cisco DMVPN Design Guide

- Dynamic Multipoint IPsec VPNs (Using Multipoint GRE/NHRP to Scale IPsec VPNs)

- DMVPN Management

- Open source NHRP protocol implementation

Chapter 11

FreeLAN

FreeLAN is an open source software application that implements peer-to-peer, full mesh, virtual private network (VPN) techniques for creating secure point-to-point or site-to-site connections in routed or bridged configurations and remote access facilities.

11.1 Encryption

FreeLAN uses the OpenSSL library to provide encryption of both the data and control channels. It lets OpenSSL do all the encryption and authentication work, allowing FreeLANto use all the ciphers available in the OpenSSL package.

11.2 Authentication

FreeLAN has several ways to authenticate peers with each other. From version 2.0 FreeLAN offers pre-shared keys, certificate-based, and username/password-based authentication.

11.3 How to make FreeLAN clients connect to each other in p2p mode

If you want to connect to someone via p2p connection, you must add his certificate to your configuration file.

For example, Alice needs to be connected to Bob directly, not through a server.

Both of them have one server in configuration contact
contact=158.88.132.221:12000

Alice's configuration file must have this line
dynamic_contact_file=c:\freelan\Bob.crt - path to Bob's certificate

Bob's configuration must NOT have this line
accept_contact_requests=no - by default this option is set yes, so you can just comment it
All of them should have relay mode on. It means server, Alice, and Bob must have this line
relay_mode_enabled=yes

11.4 References

[1] FreeLAN Change Log - FreeLAN Change Log

11.5 External links

- FreeLAN Website

Chapter 12

LogMeIn Hamachi

LogMeIn Hamachi is intended as a zero-configuration virtual private network (VPN) application that is capable of establishing direct links between computers that are behind NAT firewalls without requiring reconfiguration (when the user's PC can be accessed directly without relays from the Internet/WAN side); in other words, it establishes a connection over the Internet that emulates the connection that would exist if the computers were connected over a local area network.

It is currently available as a production version for Microsoft Windows and OS X, as a beta version for Linux, and a system-VPN-based client compatible with iOS and Android.

For paid subscribers Hamachi runs in the background on idle computers. The feature was previously available to all users, but became restricted to paid subscribers only.

12.1 Operational summary

Hamachi is a proprietary centrally-managed VPN system, consisting of the server cluster managed by the vendor of the system and the client software, which is installed on end-user computers. Client software adds a virtual network interface to a computer, and it is used for intercepting outbound as well as injecting inbound VPN traffic. Outbound traffic sent by the operating system to this interface is delivered to the client software, which encrypts and authenticates it and then sends it to the destination VPN peer over a specially initiated UDP connection. Hamachi currently handles tunneling of IP traffic including broadcasts and multicast. The Windows version also recognizes and tunnels IPX traffic.

Each client establishes and maintains a control connection to the server cluster. When the connection is established, the client goes through a login sequence, followed by the discovery process and state synchronization. The login step authenticates the client to the server and vice versa. The discovery is used to determine the topology of the client's Internet connection, specifically to detect the presence of NAT and firewall devices on its route to the Internet. The synchronization step brings a client's view of its private networks in sync with other members of these networks.

When a member of a network goes online or offline, the server instructs other network peers to either establish or tear down tunnels to the former. When establishing tunnels between the peers, Hamachi uses a server-assisted NAT traversal technique, similar to UDP hole punching. Detailed information on how it works has not been made public. This process does not work on certain combinations of NAT devices, requiring the user to explicitly set up a port forward. Additionally 1.0 series of client software are capable of relaying traffic through vendor-maintained 'relay servers'.

In the event of unexpectedly losing a connection to the server, the client retains all its tunnels and starts actively checking their status. When the *server* unexpectedly loses client's connection, it informs client's peers about the fact and expects them to also start liveliness checks. This enables Hamachi tunnels to withstand transient network problems on the route between the client and the server as well as short periods of complete server unavailability. Some Hamachi clients also get closed port on other clients, which cannot be repaired by port forwarding.

Hamachi is frequently used for gaming and remote administration. The vendor provides free basic service, and extra features for a fee.

In February 2007, an IP-level block was imposed by Hamachi servers on parts of Vietnamese Internet space due to "the scale of the system abuse originating from blocked addresses". The company is working on a less intrusive solution to the problem.

12.2 Addressing

Each Hamachi client is normally assigned an IP address when it logs into the system for the first time. To avoid conflicting with existing private networks on the client side the normal private IP address blocks 10.0.0.0/8, 172.16.0.0/12 and 192.168.0.0/16 are not used.

Before November 19, 2012 the 5.0.0.0/8 range was used. This range was previously unallocated but was allocated to RIPE NCC in late 2010 and space from this range is now being used by hosting providers on the public internet. Hamachi switched to the 25.0.0.0/8 block.[2]

The 25.0.0.0/8 block is allocated to the British Ministry of Defence. Organisations who need to communicate with the MOD may experience problems when more specific Internet routes attract traffic that was meant for internal hosts, or alternatively find themselves unable to reach the legitimate users of those addresses because those addresses are being used internally,[3] and such "squatting" is against the established practice of the Internet.

The client now supports IPv6, and if this is selected then the address assigned is picked from a range registered to LogMeIn.[2]

The IP address assigned to the Hamachi client is henceforth associated with the client's public crypto key. As long as the client retains its key, it can log into the system and use this IP address. Hamachi creates a single broadcast domain between all clients. This makes it possible to use LAN protocols that rely on IP broadcasts for discovery and announcement services over Hamachi networks.

12.3 Security

The following considerations apply to Hamachi's use as a VPN application:

- Additional risk of disclosure of sensitive data which is stored or may be logged by the mediation server — minimal where data is not forwarded.

- The security risks due to vulnerable services on remote machines otherwise not accessible behind a firewall, common to all VPNs.

- Hamachi is stated to use strong, industry-standard algorithms to secure and authenticate the data and its security architecture is open. Despite this security cannot necessarily be guaranteed.[4]

- The existing client-server protocol documentation contains a number of errors,[5][6] some of which have been confirmed by the vendor, pending correction,[7] with others not yet confirmed.

- For the product to work, a "mediation server", operated by the vendor, is required.

- This server stores the nickname, maintenance password, statically-allocated 25.0.0.0/8 IP address and the associated authentication token of the user. As such, it can potentially log actual IP addresses of the VPN users as well as various details of the session.

12.4 Compatibility

The current builds of Hamachi are available for the following operating systems:[8]

- Microsoft Windows (XP or later)

- OS X (10.6 or newer; Intel-based Macs only)

- Linux (beta)

- FreeBSD users can install and utilize Linux version, there's a port created in FreeBSD Ports.

- iOS (via iOS system VPN)

- Android (via Android system VPN)

Prior to versions 1.0.2.0 and 1.0.2.1 for the Windows release,[9] many Windows Vista users had experienced compatibility and connection issues while using Hamachi. As of March 30, 2007, the software now includes *Vista tweaks*, which answer these OS-related problems, among other specific solutions.[10]

12.5   See also

- Network address translation (NAT) Overview, related RFCs: RFC 4008, RFC 3022, RFC 1631 (obsolete)

- Simple Traversal of UDP over NATs (STUN), a NAT traversal protocol defined in RFC 3489 (obsoleted by RFC 5389)

- Session Traversal Utilities for NAT (Updated STUN, as defined in RFC 5389)

- UDP hole punching another NAT traversal technique

- Virtual Private LAN Service

- XLink Kai

- Pertino

12.6   References

[1] "Hamachi Release Notes"

[2] "Changes to Hamachi on November 19th", Official LogMeIn product blog

[3] Vegoda, Leo. "Used but Unallocated: Potentially Awkward /8 Assignments". *The Internet Protocol Journal — Volume 10, No. 3*. Cisco.com. Retrieved 2011-03-25.

[4] "LogMeIn Hamachi2 Security Whitepaper". Logmeinsupport.com. Retrieved 2011-04-12.

[5] Hamachi protocol documentation errors. Hamachi.cc forums.

[6] More Hamachi protocol documentation concerns. Hamachi.cc forums.

[7] Acknowledgement of documentation errors. Hamachi.cc forums.

[8] "FAQ: What are the system requirements for LogMeIn Hamachi?". LogMeIn, Inc. Retrieved 13 June 2015.

[9] "Hamachi for Windows, change log". Hamachi.cc. Retrieved 2011-04-12.

[10] "Hamachi Community Forums - 1.0.2.1 is released". Forums.hamachi.cc. Retrieved 2011-04-12.

12.7   External links

- Official website

- Hamachi Network List

Chapter 13

Hola (VPN)

Hola is a freemium web and mobile application which claims to provide a faster, private and more secure Internet. It provides a form of virtual private network services to its users through a peer-to-peer network. It also uses peer-to-peer caching. When a user accesses certain domains that are known to use geo-blocking, the Hola application redirects the request to go through the computers and internet connections of other users in non-blocked areas, thereby circumventing the blocking. This also means that other users might access the internet through one's own computer, and that part of one's upload bandwidth might be used for serving cached data to other users.[1][2][3][4] Paying users can choose to redirect all requests to peers but are themselves never used as peers.[5]

13.1   History

In 1998, Ofer Vilenski and Derry Shribman founded KRFTech, a software development tools company.[6] With the profits from the company, they started Jungo in 2000 to develop an operating system for home gateways. In 2006 NDS (Cisco) acquired Jungo for $107 million.[7][8]

In 2008, Vilenski and Shribman started investigating the idea of re-inventing HTTP by building a peer-to-peer overlay network that would employ peer-to-peer caching to accelerate content distribution and peer-to-peer routing to make the effective bandwidth to target sites much faster. This would make the Internet faster for users and cheaper to operate for content distributors. They started up Hola with $18 million from investors such as DFJ (Skype, Hotmail), Horizons Ventures (Mr. Li Ka-Shing's fund),[9] Magma Venture Partners (Waze), Israel's Chief Scientist Fund, and others.[10][11]

Hola Networks Limited launched their network in late 2012,[4] and it became viral in January 2013 when consumers started using Hola for Internet privacy and anonymity by utilizing the P2P routing for IP masking."After being around for two months with 80 downloads a day, on January 23rd 2013, at 5PM Israel time, the product was good enough. That was the second it took off, and went up overnight to 40,000 downloads a day", Vilenski told *Startup Camel*.[12]

In late 2014, Hola Networks began selling access to its huge userbase as exit nodes, under the name Luminati. They charge $20 per gigabyte for bandwidth that is actually coming from their VPN users—they do not pay for the bandwidth at all. Every Hola user is actually functioning as an exit node in a huge botnet.[13][14]

13.2   Architecture

The Hola company claims the following: "*The Internet is slowed down by server response times, Internet congestion, round trip times, and poorly written communication stacks in operating systems. Hola removes these bottlenecks by securely caching content on peers as they view it, and later serving it up to other nearby peers as they need it. Hola also compresses communication between peers to further speed the net.*"[15]

13.3   Platforms

Hola is distributed as a client side browser based application.[16] It is available for all major browsers such as Chrome, Firefox, Internet Explorer, Opera as browser add-on, extension, or application, and it works on PC based operating systems as well as Mac OS X.[17][18] Hola has also released an Android application[19] and most recently an iPhone and iPad application.[20][21] New downloads of the Android application were disabled on the Google Play Store on February 25, 2015.[22]

13.4   Criticism

In May 2015, Hola came under criticism from 8chan founder Frederick Brennan after the site was reportedly attacked by exploiting the Hola network, as confirmed by Hola founder Ofer Vilenski. After Brennan emailed the company, Hola modified its FAQ to include a notice that its users are acting as exit nodes for paid users of Hola's sister service Luminati. "Adios, Hola!", a website created by nine security researchers and promoted across 8chan, states: "Hola is harmful to the internet as a whole, and to its users in particular. You might know it as a free VPN or "unblocker", but in reality it operates like a poorly secured botnet - with serious consequences."[23] Much of the criticism against Hola stems from the fact that many free users are unaware that their bandwidth is being used by other users or is being resold to users of Luminati.[24]

In response to the criticism, Vilenski told *Business Insider*, "[we have been] listening to the conversations about Hola and while we think we've been clear about what we are doing, we have decided to provide more details about how this works, and thus the changes [to the website] in the past 24 hours.".[25]

In June 2015, Hola was temporarily pulled from Google's Chrome Web Store.[26] However, it remained in the Google Play Store as an Android app.[27] A few days later, on June 23, 2015, Hola browser was live again on the Chrome web store [28]

13.5   References

[1] "Sweet: Hola lets you use Hulu, Pandora, Netflix, CBS, Fox, BBC iPlayer TV, and iTV from any country". The Next Web. Retrieved 28 September 2014.

[2] "REINVENTING THE WEB: A New App Lets You Watch Whatever TV Program You Want, Including The Olympics, Anywhere In The World". Business Insider. Retrieved 28 September 2014.

[3] "Hola Unblocker Gives You Access to iPlayer, Netflix, Pandora, Hulu, and More Regardless of Region". Lifehacker. Retrieved 28 September 2014.

[4] "Unlock Hulu and BBC iPlayer in a click with Hola". The Sydney Morning Herald. Retrieved 29 September 2014.

[5] "FAQ – Hola – Is Hola Free?". *Hola*. Hola. Retrieved 2014-10-06.

[6] "Jungo Ltd. - Company Profile". *BusinessWeek*.

[7] "NDS to buy Israel's Jungo for up to $107.5 mln". *Reuters*. 4 Dec 2006.

[8] Ben-Artzi, Amir. "NDS to pay $107 million for Jungo". Electronic Engineering Times. Retrieved 28 September 2014.

[9] "The story behind a HK billionaire's $130 million donation to the Technion". Haaretz. Retrieved 28 September 2014.

[10] "Faster Internet co Hola raises $10m". Globes. Retrieved 28 September 2014.

[11] "Ofer Vilenski Co-Founder, Hola!". BusinessWeek. Retrieved 28 September 2014.

[12] "'How Hola went from 80 daily new users to 40,000 overnight with zero marketing' (interview with Ofer Vilenski, co-founder and CEO of Hola for Startup Camel Podcast". Startup Camel. Retrieved 3 June 2015.

[13] "Beware: Hola VPN turns your PC into an exit node and sells your traffic". 28 May 2015.

[14] http://www.quora.com/I-need-to-do-some-massive-web-data-collection-does-anyone-know-how-Luminati-is-different-from-Tor-or-a-proxy-n

[15] "FAQ – Hola". *Hola*. Hola. Retrieved 2014-10-06.

[16] "How to Unblock Websites: 8 Tricks That Do It". Udemy. Retrieved 28 September 2014.

[17] "The Easiest Method for Desktop: Hola Better Internet". Lifehacker. Retrieved 28 September 2014.

[18] "Running Hola on Mac OS X – Hola". *Hola*. Hola. Retrieved 2014-10-06.

[19] "Hola Lets You Watch Region-Blocked Videos From Any Country For Free". Lifehacker. Retrieved 28 September 2014.

[20] "Can I get Hola for my iPhone, iPad or iPod Touch?". Official Website. Retrieved 28 September 2014.

[21] "Hola Unblocker – Easily Access Region-Blocked Content". MakeUseOf. Retrieved 28 September 2014.

[22] "Hola Free VPN". Play Store. Retrieved 25 February 2015.

[23] "Adios, Hola! Popular privacy-minded browser plug-in has backdoor for hackers - report". *RT*. Retrieved 30 May 2015.

[24] Reddick, James. "Why Using the Hola VPN Service Is a Bad Idea". FreeVPN.me. Retrieved 18 June 2015.

[25] Price, Rob. "A wildly popular Google Chrome extension was being used as a giant botnet". *Business Insider*. Retrieved 30 May 2015.

[26] "Hola Better Internet". *Google Chrome Web Store*. Retrieved 30 May 2015.

[27] "Hola Free VPN". *Google Play*. Retrieved 30 May 2015.

[28] https://chrome.google.com/webstore/detail/hola-better-internet/gkojfkhlekighikafcpjkiklfbnlmeio

13.6 External links

- Hola Official Website

Chapter 14

Hotspot Shield

Hotspot Shield is a software application developed by AnchorFree, Inc. that allows the user to connect to a virtual private network (VPN).[5][6] It is used for securing Internet connections, often in unsecured networks.[5] Hotspot Shield was used to bypass government censorship during the Arab Spring protests in Egypt, Tunisia, and Libya.[7][8]

14.1 Overview

Hotspot Shield was developed by AnchorFree, a company in silicon valley.[5][9] The software was released in April 2008 for Windows and Mac operating systems, and was expanded to include support for iOS and Android in 2011 and 2012, respectively.[10]

Hotspot Shield establishes a virtual private network connection. The software usually protects information from being accessed or tracked by third parties.[7] AnchorFree operates Hotspot Shield with a freemium business model: the main features of the software are free, but users have to pay to get additional features, which include the elimination of advertisements, antivirus protection and the ability to choose which country from several wherein the VPN is located.

14.2 Product

Hotspot Shield encrypts data sent to the VPN to (normally) prevent successful eavesdropping.[6] Hotspot Shield also allows users to (usually) hide their IP address.[11] VPN's cannot make any user completely anonymous on the Internet, but they can greatly increase privacy and security.[12] Users can bypass censorship using Hotspot Shield by connecting to a VPN server located outside his/her country.[13]

14.3 International use

Hotspot Shield has been used to bypass Internet censorship in countries with strict Internet censorship programs.[8][14]

During the Arab Spring protests in 2010, protesters used Hotspot Shield to access social networking tools to communicate and upload videos.[8][11] Hotspot Shield was also widely used during the Egyptian protests and revolution in 2011, when the Mubarak regime cracked down heavily on access to social media sites.[15]

In 2012, Hotspot Shield usage increased among Mac users in the United States and Europe, as 500,000 Mac users were infected by the Flashback virus. Hotspot Shield was used as a protection against the virus.[16]

In 2013, usage of Hotspot Shield increased in Turkey, in response to the suspected efforts of the Turkish government to censor social media and citizen access to international websites.[17][18]

In 2014, usage of Hotspot Shield increased in Hong Kong after the outbreak of the 2014 Hong Kong protests.[19]

14.4 Critical reception

Hotspot Shield has generally received positive reviews by industry publications and websites.[20][21][22] PC Magazine rated the software "excellent" and praised its status indicator, traffic encryption, connection speed at times and payment flexibility - but criticized the software's ad platform, website code injection, slowdown of overall response time and browser setting modifications.[23] *Best VPN* lauded Hotspot Shield's value and speed, but was less enthusiastic about its features, reliability and tech support. Their review said "While Hotspot Shield does its job effectively, it probably won't appeal to technical users...".[24]

14.5 Awards and recognition

In 2013, Hotspot Shield (and AnchorFree) was awarded the Appy Award for Best Online Security/Privacy Application, as well as Softonic's 2013 Best Apps of Mobile World Congress.[25] AnchorFree was also named among the 15 most important security startups of 2013.[26]

14.6 References

[1] Hotspot Shield version history

[2] Hotspot Shield Free VPN

[3] Hotspot Shield

[4] Hotspot Shield Elite

[5] "Company Overview of AnchorFree, Inc.". *Bloomberg Businessweek*. Retrieved 25 June 2013.

[6] Empson, Rip. "With Its Hotspot Shield Hitting 60M Downloads, AnchorFree Lands A Whopping $52M From Goldman Sachs". *TechCrunch*. Retrieved 25 June 2013.

[7] Levin, Dan (16 January 2010). "Software Makers See a Market in Censorship". The New York Times. Retrieved 25 June 2013.

[8] Greene, Rachel. "Arab Spring and Emerging Technology". *CNN iReport*. Retrieved 25 June 2013.

[9] "About AnchorFree". *AnchorFree*. Retrieved 25 June 2013.

[10] "News & Events". *AnchorFree*. Retrieved 25 June 2013.

[11] Messieh, Nancy. "Hotspot Shield: A quiet hero for Internet privacy and security around the world". *TNW*. Retrieved 25 June 2013.

[12] "I am Anonymous When I Use a VPN". *goldenfrog.com*. Golden Frog. Retrieved 2015-02-24.

[13] Colao, J.J. "How To Thwart Hackers And Dictators With One Free Download". *Forbes*. Retrieved 25 June 2013.

[14] "Hotspot Shield Free VPN Experiences 1000% Growth Surge in the Wake of Recent Turkish Unrest". The Wall Street Journal. Retrieved 25 June 2013.

[15] Koehn, Josh. "AnchorFree Opens Doors to Revolution". *SanJose.com*. Retrieved 25 June 2013.

[16] "Mac virus a 'wake-up call', says CEO". *CNME*. Retrieved 25 June 2013.

[17] Ballim, Evren; Sandle, Paul (6 June 2013). "Turks skip suspected censorship with Internet lifelines". *Reuters*. Retrieved 25 June 2013.

[18] Acohido, Byron (5 June 2013). "Turkey citizens use VPN to air grievances". *USA Today*. Retrieved 25 June 2013.

[19] "Hong Kong Protests Beating the Media Crackdown". Forbes. Retrieved 26 October 2014.

[20] "The best free VPN services of 2015 for UK users: access blocked sites and surf the web anonymously". *pcadvisor.co.uk*. PC Advisor. Retrieved 2015-02-24.

[21] "Hotspot Shield Offers VPN Servers in Multiple Countries, Perfect for Watching Blocked Content Overseas". *http://lifehacker. com/*. Retrieved 2015-02-18.

[22] "Hotspot Shield Elite". *toptenreviews.com*. toptenreviews.com. Retrieved 2015-02-18.

[23] "Hotspot Shield Elite". *pcmag.com*. PC Magazine. Retrieved 2015-02-18.

[24] "Hotspot Shield Review". *bestvpn.com*. Best VPN. Retrieved 2015-02-18.

[25] Thornton, James. "The best apps of Mobile World Congress 2013". *Softonic*. Retrieved 25 June 2013.

[26] Bort, Julie. "The 15 Most Important Security Startups of 2013". *Business Insider*. Retrieved 25 June 2013.

Chapter 15

Ipredator

IPredator is a virtual private networking service offered with the stated goal of providing internet privacy.[1] It is a response to the introduction of IPRED in Sweden, which will allow copyright holders and law enforcement officials to request personal information about copyright infringement suspects.[2]

On 12 August 2009, the beta testing invitations were sent out to those who entered their email addresses into the beta signup form. Additionally, the homepage has changed to reflect the beta. The initially only used PPTP (supported natively in XP, Vista, Windows 7, OS X and GNU/Linux through the use of PPTP-linux) to tunnel the connection through servers (vpn.ipredator.se which resolves to multiple IP addresses) located in Sweden.

On September 14, 2009, IPredator "The Second Batch" became available for public consumption.

On November 28, 2009, IPredator became publicly available and exited the beta stage. This was done to counteract FRA, which started listening to internet traffic over the Swedish borders on December 1. To reflect this, The Pirate Bay changed their logo on December 1, 2009, to an image from the game Mike Tyson's Punch-Out!! depicting FRA as the opponent Glass Joe, which is a legendary easy opponent from the game. The image linked to ipredator.se with the message "FRA vs IPredator - It's on!"

On Windows clients using built-in PPTP, it is recommended to disable IPv6, File and Printer Sharing for Microsoft Networks and Client for Microsoft Networks because these features may disclose information.[3] Using OpenVPN instead has no such issues, and provides full native IPv6 connectivity.

OpenVPN support was added during August 2012.[4]

On July 2013, PayPal stopped providing payment services to Ipredator. In addition, all the organization's funds have been frozen for up to 180 days.[5]

IPredator's blog states that "PayPal reinstated our account" as of August 26, 2013.[6]

As of November 2014, the service costs SEK 50 (or $8, or €6) per month. The site accepts credit card payments via Payza and payment processors PayPal, OKPay, Payson as well as Bitcoin.[7]

15.1 Notes

[1] Horton, Michael, *Meet IPredator - Secure Anonymous VPN from Pirate Bay*, Tech Fragments, retrieved 2009-03-27

[2] Cheng, Jacqui (2009-03-26), *The Pirate Bay to roll out secure €5 per month VPN service*, Ars Technica, retrieved 2012-01-28

[3] Kaushik Patowary (2010-06-18), *Security flaw makes PPTP VPN useless for hiding IP on BitTorrent*, retrieved 2011-06-06

[4] https://blog.ipredator.se/2012/08/

[5] Andre Yoskowitz (24 July 2013). "PayPal shuts off VPN iPredator, freezes assets". *AfterDawn*. Retrieved 10 August 2013.

[6] "PayPal working again, PaySafeCard support canceled". 26 August 2013. Retrieved 10 October 2013.

[7] "IPredator - Payment". Retrieved 11 November 2014.

15.2 External links

- Official site

- More anti-IPRED software

Chapter 16

KAME project

The **KAME project** was a joint effort of six organizations in Japan which aimed to provide a free IPv6 and IPsec (for both IPv4 and IPv6) protocol stack implementation for variants of the BSD Unix computer operating-system.[1] The project began in 1998 and on November 7, 2005 it was announced that the project would be finished at the end of March 2006.[2] The name KAME is a short version of Karigome, the location of the project's offices, and it also is a word for turtles.[3]

The following organizations participated in the project:

- ALAXALA Networks Corporation

- Fujitsu, Ltd.

- Hitachi, Ltd.

- Internet Initiative Japan Inc.

- Keio University

- NEC Corporation

- University of Tokyo

- Toshiba Corporation

- Yokogawa Electric Corporation

FreeBSD, NetBSD and DragonFly BSD integrated IPSec and IPv6 code from the KAME project; OpenBSD integrated just IPv6 code rather than both (having developed their own IPSec stack). Linux also integrated code from the project in its native IPsec implementation.[4]

The KAME project collaborated with the TAHI Project (which develops and provides verification-technology for IPv6), the USAGI Project and the WIDE Project.

16.1 Racoon

racoon, KAME's user-space daemon, handles Internet Key Exchange (IKE). In Linux systems it forms part of the ipsec-tools package.

16.2   References

[1] Hagen 2006, p. 346.

[2] http://www.kame.net/newsletter/20051107/

[3] http://playground.iijlab.net/material/kazu-kame-presen/mgp00015.html

[4] Roy, Vincent (12 October 2004), *Benchmarks for Native IPsec in the 2.6 Kernel*, Linux Journal

- Hagen, Silvia. *IPv6 Essentials*. O'Reilly Media. ISBN 9780596553418. Retrieved 5 June 2014.

16.3   External links

- Official website

- ALAXALA Networks Corporation

- Internet Initiative Japan Inc.

- NetBSD manual page for Racoon

- IPsec-Tools, a port of KAME's IPsec utilities to the Linux-2.6 IPsec implementation

Chapter 17

Kerio Control

Kerio Control (previously called **Kerio WinRoute Firewall** and before that **WinRoute Pro**) is a unified threat management solution developed by Kerio Technologies (earlier known as Tiny Software). It includes a VPN server, an integrated Sophos anti-virus (optional), a firewall, web filtering, a bandwidth limiter, Internet an monitor and user-specific Internet access management. Kerio Control runs Linux, providing network perimeter defense for small to medium organizations. Kerio Control 7.6 was the last version to run on Microsoft Windows.[1]

17.1 Release history

17.2 See also

- Personal firewall

- Tiny Software

- Kerio Technologies

17.3 References

[1] Gudeli, James (31 October 2012). "The Metamorphosis - Kerio Control 7.4 will be last version on Windows". *Kerio Blog*. Kerio Technologies.

[2] "WinRoute Pro - A proxy server with built-in router, firewall, and e-mail services —". Serverwatch.com. 2000-09-14. Retrieved 2010-07-08.

17.4 External links

- Official website

- PC Magazine review of Kerio WinRoute Firewall 6.5

- http://pymeapps.com/kerio/control

Chapter 18

Layer 2 Tunneling Protocol

In computer networking, **Layer 2 Tunnelling Protocol** (**L2TP**) is a tunnelling protocol used to support virtual private networks (VPNs) or as part of the delivery of services by ISPs. It does not provide any encryption or confidentiality by itself. Rather, it relies on an encryption protocol that it passes within the tunnel to provide privacy.[1]

18.1 History

Published in 1999 as proposed standard RFC 2661, L2TP has its origins primarily in two older tunnelling protocols for point-to-point communication: Cisco's Layer 2 Forwarding Protocol (L2F) and Microsoft's[2] Point-to-Point Tunnelling Protocol (PPTP). A new version of this protocol, L2TPv3, appeared as proposed standard RFC 3931 in 2005. L2TPv3 provides additional security features, improved encapsulation, and the ability to carry data links other than simply Point-to-Point Protocol (PPP) over an IP network (for example: Frame Relay, Ethernet, ATM, etc.).

18.2 Description

The entire L2TP packet, including payload and L2TP header, is sent within a User Datagram Protocol (UDP) datagram. It is common to carry PPP sessions within an L2TP tunnel. L2TP does not provide confidentiality or strong authentication by itself. IPsec is often used to secure L2TP packets by providing confidentiality, authentication and integrity. The combination of these two protocols is generally known as L2TP/IPsec (discussed below).

The two endpoints of an L2TP tunnel are called the *LAC* (*L2TP Access Concentrator*) and the *LNS* (*L2TP Network Server*). The L2TP waits for new tunnels. Once a tunnel is established, the network traffic between the peers is bidirectional. To be useful for networking, higher-level protocols are then run through the L2TP tunnel. To facilitate this, an L2TP *session* (or '**call**') is established within the tunnel for each higher-level protocol such as PPP. Either the LAC or LNS may initiate sessions. The traffic for each session is isolated by L2TP, so it is possible to set up multiple virtual networks across a single tunnel. MTU should be considered when implementing L2TP.

The packets exchanged within an L2TP tunnel are categorized as either *control packets* or *data packets*. L2TP provides reliability features for the control packets, but no reliability for data packets. Reliability, if desired, must be provided by the nested protocols running within each session of the L2TP tunnel.

L2TP allows the creation of a virtual private dialup network (VPDN)[3] to connect a remote client to its corporate network by using a shared infrastructure, which could be the Internet or a service provider's network.

18.3 Tunneling models

An L2TP tunnel can extend across an entire PPP session or only across one segment of a two-segment session. This can be represented by four different tunneling models, namely:

- voluntary tunnel

- compulsory tunnel — incoming call

- compulsory tunnel — remote dial

- L2TP multihop connection[4]

18.4 L2TP packet structure

An L2TP packet consists of :

Field meanings:

Flags and version control flags indicating data/control packet and presence of length, sequence, and offset fields.

Length (optional) Total length of the message in bytes, present only when length flag is set.

Tunnel ID Indicates the identifier for the control connection.

Session ID Indicates the identifier for a session within a tunnel.

Ns (optional) sequence number for this data or control message, beginning at zero and incrementing by one (modulo 2^{16}) for each message sent. Present only when sequence flag set.

Nr (optional) sequence number for expected message to be received. Nr is set to the Ns of the last in-order message received plus one (modulo 2^{16}). In data messages, Nr is reserved and, if present (as indicated by the S bit), MUST be ignored upon receipt..

Offset Size (optional) Specifies where payload data is located past the L2TP header. If the offset field is present, the L2TP header ends after the last byte of the offset padding. This field exists if the offset flag is set.

Offset Pad (optional) Variable length, as specified by the offset size. Contents of this field are undefined.

Payload data Variable length (Max payload size = Max size of UDP packet − size of L2TP header)

18.5 L2TP packet exchange

At the time of setup of L2TP connection, many control packets are exchanged between server and client to establish tunnel and session for each direction. One peer requests the other peer to assign a specific tunnel and session id through these control packets. Then using this tunnel and session id, data packets are exchanged with the compressed PPP frames as payload.

The list of L2TP Control messages exchanged between LAC and LNS, for handshaking before establishing a tunnel and session in voluntary tunnelling method are

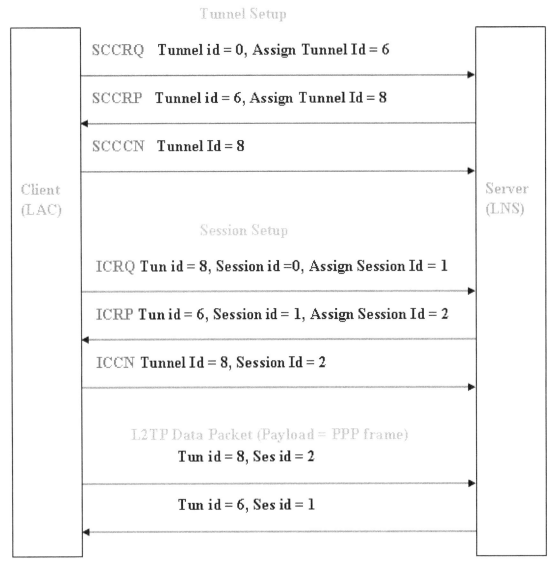

L2TP Control and Data Packets

18.6 L2TP/IPsec

Because of the lack of confidentiality inherent in the L2TP protocol, it is often implemented along with IPsec. This is referred to as L2TP/IPsec, and is standardized in IETF RFC 3193. The process of setting up an L2TP/IPsec VPN is as follows:

1. Negotiation of IPsec security association (SA), typically through *Internet key exchange* (IKE). This is carried out over UDP port 500, and commonly uses either a shared password (so-called "pre-shared keys"), public keys, or X.509 certificates on both ends, although other keying methods exist.

2. Establishment of Encapsulating Security Payload (ESP) communication in transport mode. The IP protocol number for ESP is 50 (compare TCP's 6 and UDP's 17). At this point, a secure channel has been established, but no tunnelling is taking place.

3. Negotiation and establishment of L2TP tunnel between the SA endpoints. The actual negotiation of parameters takes place over the SA's secure channel, within the IPsec encryption. L2TP uses UDP port 1701.

When the process is complete, L2TP packets between the endpoints are encapsulated by IPsec. Since the L2TP packet itself is wrapped and hidden within the IPsec packet, no information about the internal private network can be garnered from the encrypted packet. Also, it is not necessary to open UDP port 1701 on firewalls between the endpoints, since the inner packets are not acted upon until after IPsec data has been decrypted and stripped, which only takes place at the endpoints.

A potential point of confusion in L2TP/IPsec is the use of the terms **tunnel** and **secure channel**. The term **tunnel** refers to a channel which allows untouched packets of one network to be transported over another network. In the case of L2TP/PPP, it allows L2TP/PPP packets to be transported over IP. A **secure channel** refers to a connection within which the confidentiality of all data is guaranteed. In L2TP/IPsec, first IPsec provides a secure channel, then L2TP provides a tunnel.

18.7 Windows implementation

Windows Vista provides two new configuration utilities that attempt to make using L2TP without IPsec easier, both described in sections that follow below:

- an MMC snap-in called "Windows Firewall with Advanced Security"WFwAS), located in Control Panel → Administrative Tools

- the "netsh advfirewall" command-line tool

Both these configuration utilities are not without their difficulties, and unfortunately, there is very little documentation about both "netsh advfirewall" and the IPsec client in WFwAS. One of the aforementioned difficulties is that it is not compatible with NAT. Another problem is that servers must be specified only by IP address in the new Vista configuration utilities; the hostname of the server cannot be used, so if the IP address of the IPsec server changes, all clients will have to be informed of this new IP address (which also rules out servers that addressed by utilities such as DynDNS).

18.8 L2TP in ISPs' networks

L2TP is often used by ISPs when internet service over for example ADSL or cable is being *resold*. From the end user, packets travel over a wholesale network service provider's network to a server called a Broadband Remote Access Server (BRAS), a protocol converter and router combined. On legacy networks the path from end user customer premises' equipment to the BRAS may be over an ATM network. From there on, over an IP network, an L2TP tunnel runs from the BRAS (acting as LAC) to an LNS which is an edge router at the boundary of the ultimate destination ISP's IP network. See example of reseller ISPs using L2TP.

18.9 See also

- IPsec

- Layer 2 Forwarding Protocol

- Point-to-Point Tunnelling Protocol

- Point-to-Point Protocol

- Shortest Path Bridging

18.10   References

[1] IETF (1999), RFC 2661, Layer Two Tunnelling Protocol "L2TP"

[2] "Point-to-Point Tunnelling Protocol (PPTP)". TheNetworkEncyclopedia.com. 2013. Retrieved 2014-07-28. Point-to-Point Tunnelling Protocol (PPTP) [:] A data-link layer protocol for wide area networks (WANs) based on the Point-to-Point Protocol (PPP) and developed by Microsoft that enables network traffic to be encapsulated and routed over an unsecured public network such as the Internet.

[3] http://www.cisco.com/en/US/tech/tk801/tk703/technologies_tech_note09186a0080094586.shtml

[4] http://publib.boulder.ibm.com/infocenter/iseries/v7r1m0/index.jsp?topic=%2Frzaiy%2Frzaiymultihop.htm

18.11   External links

18.11.1   Implementations

- Cisco: Cisco L2TP documentation, also read Technology brief from Cisco

- Open source and Linux: xl2tpd, Linux RP-L2TP, OpenL2TP, l2tpns, l2tpd (inactive), Linux L2TP/IPsec server, FreeBSD multi-link PPP daemon, OpenBSD npppd(8), ACCEL-PPP - PPTP/L2TP/PPPoE server for Linux

- Microsoft: built-in client included with Windows 2000 and higher; Microsoft L2TP/IPsec VPN Client for Windows 98/Windows Me/Windows NT 4.0

- Apple: built-in client included with Mac OS X 10.3 and higher.

- VPDN on Cisco.com

18.11.2   Internet standards and extensions

- RFC 2341 *Cisco Layer Two Forwarding (Protocol) "L2F"* (a predecessor to L2TP)

- RFC 2637 *Point-to-Point Tunnelling Protocol (PPTP)* (a predecessor to L2TP)

- RFC 2661 *Layer Two Tunnelling Protocol "L2TP"*

- RFC 2809 *Implementation of L2TP Compulsory Tunnelling via RADIUS*

- RFC 2888 *Secure Remote Access with L2TP*

- RFC 3070 *Layer Two Tunnelling Protocol (L2TP) over Frame Relay*

- RFC 3145 *L2TP Disconnect Cause Information*

- RFC 3193 *Securing L2TP using IPsec*

- RFC 3301 *Layer Two Tunnelling Protocol (L2TP): ATM access network*

- RFC 3308 *Layer Two Tunnelling Protocol (L2TP) Differentiated Services*

- RFC 3355 *Layer Two Tunnelling Protocol (L2TP) Over ATM Adaptation Layer 5 (AAL5)*

- RFC 3371 *Layer Two Tunnelling Protocol "L2TP" Management Information Base*

- RFC 3437 *Layer Two Tunnelling Protocol Extensions for PPP Link Control Protocol Negotiation*

- RFC 3438 *Layer Two Tunnelling Protocol (L2TP) Internet Assigned Numbers: Internet Assigned Numbers Authority (IANA) Considerations Update*

- RFC 3573 *Signaling of Modem-On-Hold status in Layer 2 Tunnelling Protocol (L2TP)*

- RFC 3817 *Layer 2 Tunnelling Protocol (L2TP) Active Discovery Relay for PPP over Ethernet (PPPoE)*

- RFC 3931 *Layer Two Tunnelling Protocol - Version 3 (L2TPv3)*

- RFC 4045 *Extensions to Support Efficient Carrying of Multicast Traffic in Layer-2 Tunnelling Protocol (L2TP)*

- RFC 4951 *Fail Over Extensions for Layer 2 Tunnelling Protocol (L2TP) "failover"*

18.11.3   Other

- IANA assigned numbers for L2TP

- L2TP Extensions Working Group (l2tpext) - *(where future standardization work is being coordinated)*

- Using Linux as an L2TP/IPsec VPN client

- L2TP/IPSec with OpenBSD and npppd

Chapter 19

Libreswan

In the field of computer security, Libreswan is a fork of the Openswan IPSEC VPN implementation created by almost all of the openswan developers after a lawsuit about the ownership of the Openswan name was filed against Paul Wouters, the release manager of Openswan, in December 2012.[3][4] The Libreswan project has an active community of developers and contributors with regular releases. They can be found on the #swan channel on the Freenode IRC service helping people with both libreswan and openswan problems.

19.1 External links

- Libreswan website

19.2 References

[1] "CHANGES". Retrieved 2015-09-28.

[2] "LICENSE". Retrieved 2015-09-28.

[3] Wouters, Paul (2012-12-15). "Resignation from Openswan". Retrieved 2015-09-28.

[4] Wouters, Paul (2012-12-16). "My resignation of The Openswan Project". Retrieved 2015-09-28.

Chapter 20

n2n

n2n is an open source Layer 2 over Layer 3 VPN application which utilises a peer-to-peer architecture for network membership and routing.

Unlike many other VPN programs, n2n can also connect computers which reside behind NAT routers. These connections are set up with help from a third computer that both computers can reach. This computer, called a supernode, can then route the information between *NATed* nodes.[1]

It is free software licensed under the terms of the GNU General Public License v3.

20.1 References

[1] http://www.ntop.org/products/n2n/ : "[the supernode] is basically a directory register and a packet router for those nodes that cannot talk directly"

20.2 External links

- n2n home page
- n2n on Google Play

Chapter 21

Network Extrusion

A network extrusion is a kind of VPN tunnel where a subnet (or host) is moved to another location, without any router advertisement changes. Such a subnet is routed to normally, but then send via a VPN tunnel to appear anywhere else on the internet. This type of VPN connection is often used for:

- Adding IPv4 public address space to a location that has only 1 public IP address, such as a consumer internet connection

- Assigning a static IP address to a roaming laptop to ensure it is always reachable on 1 static IP address. This is often done with IPsec and L2TP or XAUTH

In IPsec/Openswan IPv4 configuration, this corresponds to a policy on the client system like:

conn mylaptop—extruded right=192.1.0.1 rightsubnet=0.0.0.0/0 left=%defaultroute leftsubnet=192.0.0.1/32 leftsourceip=192.0.0.1

When this IPsec connection is active, the default IP address for outgoing connections is 192.0.0.1. Since this is covered by the IPsec tunnel, the packet will be encrypted and send to the remote IPsec gateway at 192.1.0.1. It will get decrypted and then sent to its original destination. Response packets follow a similar path in reverse.

When using leftsubnet=192.0.0.0/24, one could even run a small network with the laptop as default gateway and provide public IP addresses to many computers, all appearing to live at the remote site.

Generally, IPsec VPNs are used in many cases to route private networks rather than public ones, so while this configuration is not implausible, it is unusual for VPN administrators.

Many remote access situations run as network extrusions so that a corporate firewall can inspect the traffic that travels to and from the laptop computer.

This technique can also be used to tunnel in IPv6 space into networks where only IPv4 space is available (or vice versa)

These tunnels are invisible to traceroute because the IPsec tunnel appears as a single additional hop, just like a subnet.\

Chapter 22

OpenConnect

In computer networking, **OpenConnect** - an open-source software application - implements virtual private network (VPN) techniques for setting up secure point-to-point connections. It started as a client for Cisco's AnyConnect SSL VPN, which is supported by several Cisco routers, but as of 2013 it includes a server[3] and can offer a full VPN solution.

22.1 Architecture

OpenConnect uses a protocol compatible with AnyConnect's SSL protocol,[4][5] implemented within an open-source project unaffiliated with Cisco. AnyConnect VPNs utilize TLS and DTLS to encrypt and authenticate the encapsulated VPN traffic.[6]

22.2 Platforms

It is available on Solaris, Linux, OpenBSD, FreeBSD, Mac OS X, and has graphical user interface clients for Windows 2000/XP/Vista/7,[7] GNOME,[8] and KDE.[9] It is also available on mobile clients like Android devices,[10] and has been integrated into router firmware packages such as OpenWrt.[11]

22.3 References

[1] infradead.org - OpenConnect: Changelog

[2] infradead.org - OpenConnect: Changelog

[3] http://www.infradead.org/ocserv/

[4] Tiso, John; Scholfield, Mark D.; Teare, Diane (2011). *Designing Cisco Network Service Architectures (ARCH): Foundation Learning Guide*. Foundation Learning Guides (3 ed.). Cisco Press. p. 464. ISBN 9781587142888. Retrieved 2013-06-13. Cisco AnyConnect is a Cisco implementation of the thick client. Because the SSL VPN network extension runs on top of the SSL protocol, it is simpler to manage and has greater robustness with different network topologies such as firewalls and Network Address Translation (NAT) than the higher security of IPsec.

[5] "The OpenConnect VPN Protocol Version 1.0". github.com. Retrieved 2015-04-29.

[6] http://nmav.gnutls.org/2013/11/inside-ssl-vpn-protocol.html

[7] "Openconnect graphical client". GitHub. Retrieved 2014-10-28.

[8] "NetworkManager". gnome.org. Retrieved 2014-10-28.

[9] "NetworkManagement". kde.org. Retrieved 2014-10-28.

[10] cernekee. "Android UI for OpenConnect VPN client". GitHub. Retrieved 2014-10-28.

[11] "VPN Overview". Wiki.openwrt.org. Retrieved 2014-10-28.

22.4   External links

- Openconnect project homepage

Chapter 23

Openswan

In the field of computer security, **Openswan** provides a complete IPsec implementation for Linux 2.0, 2.2, 2.4 and 2.6 kernels.

Openswan, begun as a fork of the now-defunct FreeS/WAN project, continues to use the GNU General Public License. Unlike the FreeS/WAN project, it does not exclusively target the GNU/Linux operating system.

Libreswan forked from Openswan in 2012.

23.1 External links

- Openswan website
- Openswan on GitHub

23.2 References

[1] v2.6.45 on GitHub

Chapter 24

OpenVPN

OpenVPN is an open-source software application that implements virtual private network (VPN) techniques for creating secure point-to-point or site-to-site connections in routed or bridged configurations and remote access facilities. It uses a custom security protocol[3] that utilizes SSL/TLS for key exchange. It is capable of traversing network address translators (NATs) and firewalls. It was written by James Yonan and is published under the GNU General Public License (GPL).[4]

OpenVPN allows peers to authenticate each other using a pre-shared secret key, certificates, or username/password. When used in a multiclient-server configuration, it allows the server to release an authentication certificate for every client, using signature and Certificate authority. It uses the OpenSSL encryption library extensively, as well as the SSLv3/TLSv1 protocol, and contains many security and control features.

OpenVPN has been ported and embedded to several systems. For example, DD-WRT has the OpenVPN server function. SoftEther VPN, a multi-protocol VPN server, has an implementation of OpenVPN protocol.

24.1 Architecture

24.1.1 Encryption

OpenVPN uses the OpenSSL library to provide encryption of both the data and control channels. It lets OpenSSL do all the encryption and authentication work, allowing OpenVPN to use all the ciphers available in the OpenSSL package. It can also use the HMAC packet authentication feature to add an additional layer of security to the connection (referred to as an "HMAC Firewall" by the creator). It can also use hardware acceleration to get better encryption performance.[5][6] Support for PolarSSL is available starting from version 2.3.[7]

24.1.2 Authentication

OpenVPN has several ways to authenticate peers with each other. OpenVPN offers pre-shared keys, certificate-based, and username/password-based authentication. Preshared secret key is the easiest, with certificate based being the most robust and feature-rich. In version 2.0 username/password authentications can be enabled, both with or without certificates. However to make use of username/password authentications, OpenVPN depends on third-party modules. See the Extensibility paragraph for more info.

24.1.3 Networking

OpenVPN can run over User Datagram Protocol (UDP) or Transmission Control Protocol (TCP) transports, multiplexing created SSL tunnels on a single TCP/UDP port[8] (RFC 3948 for UDP).[9] From 2.3.x series on, OpenVPN fully supports IPv6 as protocol of the virtual network inside a tunnel and the OpenVPN applications can also establish connections via IPv6.[10] It has the ability to work through most proxy servers (including HTTP) and is good at working through Network address translation (NAT) and getting out through firewalls. The server configuration has the ability to "push" certain network configuration options to the clients. These include IP addresses, routing commands, and a few connection options. OpenVPN offers two types of interfaces for networking via the Universal TUN/TAP driver. It can create either a layer-3 based IP tunnel (TUN), or a layer-2 based Ethernet TAP that can carry any type of Ethernet traffic. OpenVPN can optionally use the LZO compression library to compress the data stream. Port 1194 is the official IANA assigned port number for OpenVPN. Newer versions of the program now default to that port. A feature in the 2.0 version allows for one process to manage several simultaneous tunnels, as opposed to the original "one tunnel per process" restriction on the 1.x series.

OpenVPN's use of common network protocols (TCP and UDP) makes it a desirable alternative to IPsec in situations where an ISP may block specific VPN protocols in order to force users to subscribe to a higher-priced, "business grade," service tier.

24.1.4 Security

OpenVPN offers several internal security features. It has up to 256-bit Encryption through OpenSSL library although some service providers may offer lower rates effectively making the connection faster.[11] It runs in userspace, instead of requiring IP stack (and therefore kernel) operation. OpenVPN has the ability to drop root privileges, use mlockall to prevent swapping sensitive data to disk, enter a chroot jail after initialization and apply a SELinux context after initialization.

OpenVPN runs a custom security protocol based on SSL and TLS.[3] OpenVPN offers support of smart cards via PKCS#11 based cryptographic tokens.

24.1.5 Extensibility

OpenVPN can be extended with third-party plug-ins or scripts which can be called at defined entry points.[12][13] The purpose of this is often to extend OpenVPN with more advanced logging, enhanced authentication with username and passwords, dynamic firewall updates, RADIUS integration and so on. The plug-ins are dynamically loadable modules, usually written in C, while the scripts interface can execute any scripts or binaries available to OpenVPN. In the OpenVPN source code[14] there are some examples of such plug-ins, including a PAM authentication plug-in. Several third party plug-ins also exist to authenticate against LDAP or SQL databases such as SQLite and MySQL. There is an overview over many of these extensions in the related project wiki page for the OpenVPN community.

24.2 Platforms

It is available on Solaris, Linux, OpenBSD, FreeBSD, NetBSD, QNX, Mac OS X, and Windows 2000/XP/Vista/7/8.[15] While some mobile phone OSes (Palm OS, etc.) do not support OpenVPN, it is available for Maemo,[16] Windows Mobile 6.5 and below,[17] iOS 3GS+ devices,[18] jailbroken iOS 3.1.2+ devices,[19] Android 4.0+ devices, and Android devices that have had the Cyanogenmod aftermarket firmware flashed[20] or have the correct kernel module installed.[21] It is not a "web-based" VPN, meaning that it is not shown as a web page such as Citrix or Terminal Services Web access - the program is installed independently and configured by editing text files manually, rather than through a GUI-based wizard. OpenVPN is not compatible with IPsec or any other VPN package. The entire package consists of one binary for both client and server connections, an optional configuration file, and one or more key files depending on the authentication method used.

24.2.1 Firmware implementations

OpenVPN has been integrated into router firmware packages such as Vyatta, pfSense, DD-WRT,[22] OpenWrt[23] and Tomato,[24][25] allowing users to run OpenVPN in client or server mode from their network routers. A router running

OpenVPN in client mode, for example, facilitates users within that network to access their VPN without having to install OpenVPN on each computer on that network.

OpenVPN has also been implemented in some default manufacturer router firmware, such as the D-Link DSR-250[26] and all recent MikroTik Routers.[27] MikroTik's implementation does not support the UDP protocol (as well as LZO compression), but only the TCP protocol, which has a negative impact on transfer speeds. MikroTik claims that they won't continue to improve their OpenVPN implementation (i.e. add UDP support): "It was said before - we have stopped developing OpenVPN in favor of SSTP" [28]

24.2.2 Software implementations

OpenVPN has been integrated into SoftEther VPN, an open-source multi-protocol VPN server, to allow users connect to the VPN server from existing OpenVPN clients.

24.3 Community

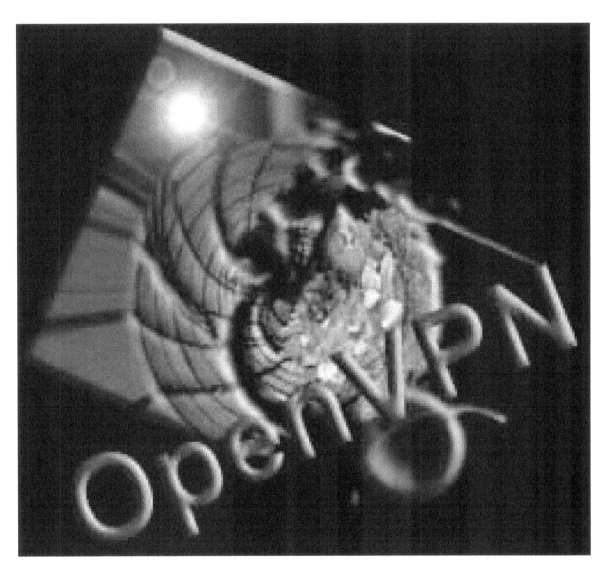

A circa 2005 version of the OpenVPN community logo.

There are many support options for OpenVPN. The primary method for community support is through the OpenVPN mailing lists. Other sources of support, not directly affiliated with OpenVPN include:

24.4   See also

- OpenConnect, implements a TLS and DTLS-based VPN

- OpenSSH, which also implements a level-2/3 "tun"-based VPN

- stunnel encrypt any TCP connection (single port service) over SSL

- UDP hole punching, a technique for establishing UDP "connections" between firewalled/NATed network nodes

- Point-to-Point Tunneling Protocol (PPTP) Microsoft method for implementing VPN

- Secure Socket Tunneling Protocol (SSTP) Microsoft method for implementing PPP over SSL VPN

- BartVPN, a VPN client implementing OpenVPN

- SoftEther VPN, an open-source VPN server program which supports OpenVPN protocol

24.5   References

[1] OpenVPN Change Log - OpenVPN Change Log

[2] https://community.openvpn.net/openvpn/wiki/ChangesInOpenvpn23

[3] "OpenVPN Security Overview". Retrieved 28 September 2011.

[4] LinuxSecurity.com - OpenVPN: An Introduction and Interview with Founder, James Yonan

[5] Network security hacks By Andrew Lockhart - Hack #104 - Create a Cross-platform VPN

[6] IPv6 Deployment Guide By 6net - Chapter 5 - Integration and Transition

[7] Overview of changes in OpenVPN v2.3 - ChangesInOpenvpn23 - OpenVPN Community

[8] OpenVPN man page, section "TLS Mode Options"

[9] User Centric Media: First International Conference, UCMedia 2009, Venice, Italy, December 9–11, 2009, Revised Selected Papers By Patros Daras, Oscar Mayora Ibarra - Scalable IPTV Delivery to Home via VPN - Proposed Scheme

[10] OpenVPN community wiki, IPv6 in OpenVPN - retrieved 2013-12-08

[11] "VPN Newbie Guide: Picking between OpenVPN, PPTP and L2TP". vpnpick.com. Retrieved 2014-03-30.

[12] "OpenVPN script entry points". Openvpn.net. Retrieved 2012-07-30.

[13] OpenVPN plug-in entry points for C based modules

[14] "OpenVPN example plug-ins". Openvpn.git.sourceforge.net. Retrieved 2012-07-30.

[15] "Downloads". *openvpn.net*. OpenVPN. Retrieved 6 August 2015.

[16] "OpenVPN Maemo package". Maemo.org. Retrieved 2012-07-30.

[17] "OpenVPN for PocketPC". Ovpnppc.ziggurat29.com. 2007-04-01. Retrieved 2012-07-30.

[18] "OpenVPN Connect". OpenVPN Technologies. 2013-01-16. Retrieved 2013-01-16.

[19] "GuizmOVPN - OpenVPN GUI for iPhone/iPad". guizmovpn.com. 2007-09-30. Retrieved 2012-09-30.

[20] cyanogen (7 July 2010). "CHANGELOG at eclair from CyanogenMod's android_vendor_cyanogen". GitHub. Retrieved 28 October 2010. Nexus One Cyanogenmod changelog

[21] "How to setup and configure OpenVPN on Android rooted device | VPN blog is actual information about VPN". Vpnblog.info. Retrieved 2012-07-30.

[22] dd-wrt.com - OpenVPN

[23] "Easy OpenVPN server setup guide - OpenWrt Wiki". Wiki.openwrt.org. Retrieved 2012-07-30.

[24] "TomatoVPN". Tomatovpn.keithmoyer.com. Retrieved 2012-07-30.

[25] LinksysInfo.org – VPN build with Web GUI

[26] http://www.dlink.com/us/en/business-solutions/security/services-routers/-/media/Business_Products/DSR/DSR%20250/Manual/ DSR%20250_Manual_104_EN_US.pdf

[27] http://wiki.mikrotik.com/wiki/OpenVPN

[28] http://forum.mikrotik.com/viewtopic.php?f=2&t=46133

24.6   External links

- OpenVPN project homepage

- OpenVPN presentation and demonstration video Hampshire Linux User Group. Archive.org. details.

Chapter 25

Private Internet Access

Private Internet Access (PIA) is a lightweight, personal VPN service that hides a user's online activity from eavesdroppers by passing data through an encrypted tunnel. It supports multiple VPN technologies such as PPTP, L2TP/IPSec, SOCKS5 and OpenVPN.[1] Private Internet Access was named PC Magazine's Editor's Choice in 2013[2] and offers several features:[3]

- DNS Leak Protection

- IPv6 Leak Protection

- Internet kill switch

- Access via UDP/TCP

- Multiple VPN Gateways

- Unlimited Bandwidth

- Port Forwarding

The CEO of Private Internet Access (and its parent company, London Trust Media, Inc) is Andrew Lee.[4]

25.1   References

[1] Deirdre Murphy (2014-07-16) Privateinternetaccess Review, VPN Critic

[2] Fahmida Rashid (2013-01-29) Private Internet Access, PCMag

[3] Melanie Pinola (2013-04-05) Grab Private Internet Access VPN Service for 20% Off, Lifehacker

[4] "Leaked: Just before Bitcoin catastrophe, MtGox dreamed of riches". *Ars Technica*.

25.2   External links

- Official website

- Private Internet Access Reviews

Chapter 26

Social VPN

A **social VPN** is a virtual private network that is created among individual peers, automatically, based on relationships established by them through a social networking service. A social VPN aims at providing peer-to-peer (P2P) network connectivity between a user and his or her friends, in an easy to set up manner that hides from the users the complexity in setting up and maintaining authenticated/encrypted end-to-end VPN tunnels.

26.1 Architecture

An architecture of a social VPN is based on a centralized infrastructure where users authenticate, discover their friends and exchange cryptographic public keys, and a P2P overlay which is used to route messages between VPN endpoints.[1] The approach is

26.1.1 Packet capture and injection

A social VPN uses a virtual network interface (such as TUN/TAP devices in Windows and Unix systems) to capture and inject IP packets from a host. Once captured, packets are encrypted, encapsulated, and routed over an overlay network.

26.1.2 Security

A social VPN uses online social networks to distribute public keys and advertise node address to friends. The acquired public keys are used to establish encrypted communication between two endpoints. Symmetric keys are exchanged during the process of establishing an end-to-end link by two social VPN peers.

26.1.3 Routing

Routing in the social VPN is peer-to-peer. One approach that has been implemented uses a structured P2P system for sending IP packets encapsulated in overlay messages from a source to destination.

26.1.4 Private IP address space

A social VPN uses dynamic IP address assignment and translation to avoid collision with existing (private) address spaces of end hosts, and to allow the system to scale to the number of users that today's successful online social network services serve (tens of millions). Users are able to connect directly only to a small subset of the total number of users of such a service, where the subset is determined by their established relationships.

26.1.5 Naming

A social VPN uses names derived from the social network service to automatically assign host names to endpoints. These names are translated to virtual private IP addresses in the overlay by a loop-back DNS virtual server.

26.2 Related systems

- The MIT Unmanaged Internet Architecture[2] (UIA)provides *ad hoc*, zero-configuration routing infrastructure for mobile devices, but the *ad hoc* connections are not established through a social networking infrastructure.[3]

- "Friend Net" is a similar concept put forth in a 2002 blog entry.[4]

- Hamachi is a zero-configuration VPN which uses a security architecture different from that of social VPN.[5] The leafnetworks VPN also supports the creation of networks using the Facebook API.

26.3 Software

An open-source social VPN implementation based on the Facebook social network service and the Brunet P2P overlay is available for Windows and Linux systems under MIT license. It creates direct point-to-point secure connections between computers with the help of online social networks, and supports transparent traversal of NATs. It uses the P2P overlay to create direct VPN connections between pairs of computers (nodes). To establish a connection, two nodes advertise their P2P node address (as well as public keys for secure communication) to each other through an online social network. Once each node acquires the node address (and public keys) of the other node, an IP-to-nodeAddress mapping is created and IP packets can be routed through the VPN tunnel.

26.4 References

[1] R. Figueiredo, P. O. Boykin, P. St. Juste, D. Wolinsky, "SocialVPNs: Integrating Overlay and Social Networks for Seamless P2P Networking", in Proceedings of IEEE WETICE/COPS, Rome, Italy, June 2008.

[2] Unmanaged Internet Architecture

[3] Bryan Ford, Jacob Strauss, Chris Lesniewski-Laas, Sean Rhea, Frans Kaashoek, and Robert Morris, "Persistent Personal Names for Globally Connected Mobile Devices", in Proceedings of the 7th USENIX Symposium on Operating Systems Design and Implementation (OSDI '06), Seattle, WA, November 2006.

[4] Lucas Gonze "Friendnet", blog entry (2002-12-15). Retrieved on 2008-09-23.

[5] LogMeIn Hamachi Security Architecture.

26.5 External links

- socialvpn.org
- We Are Hidden, Social VPN

Chapter 27

SoftEther Corporation

This article is about a Japanese company. For an open-source VPN software, see SoftEther VPN.

SoftEther Corporation is a Japanese software company. It was founded as an industry-academia-government venture in April 2004 by University of Tsukuba students, with the goal to develop the software of the same name, SoftEther VPN. The name indicated that a *soft*ware emulates an *Ether*net.

27.1 Related software

27.1.1 SoftEther

The VPN software called **SoftEther** (**SoftEther 1.0**) was written by Daiyu Nobori, who became the Representative Director and Chairman of the new company. In 2003, the software's development was adopted as one of the projects of the Exploratory Youth program, sponsored by Information Technology Promotion Agency, Japan. "In addition to being highly evaluated by the project manager, there were 1 million downloads in three months after making it available at the website."[1]

The first SoftEther sales version was released in August 2004 called **SoftEther CA**, by Mitsubishi Materials Corporation, Japan.

27.1.2 PacketiX VPN

The second version of the software, released in December 2005, the name of the software was changed to **PacketiX VPN 2.0** from **SoftEther 2.0**. In 2006, PacketiX VPN 2.0 won the "Software of the Year" award from the Information-Technology Promotion Agency.

In 2010 March, **PacketiX VPN 3.0** was released by Softether Corporation. Some functions were added to new version (as examples: support IPv6, 802.1Q VLAN, TLS 1.0).[2] This version is compatible with PacketiX VPN 2.0.[3]

In 2013 July, **PacketiX VPN 4.0** was released by SoftEther Corporation. In this version, some existent protocols support was added.[4]

27.1.3 UT-VPN

Main article: UT-VPN

In 2010 June, UT-VPN was released by SoftEther Corporation and University of Tsukuba. UT-VPN is an open source VPN software. UT-VPN has compatible as PacketiX VPN products of SoftEther Corporation.

UT-VPN developed based on PacketiX VPN 3.0, but some functions was deleted. For example, the RADIUS client is supported by PacketiX VPN Server, but it is not supported by UT-VPN Server.

27.1.4 SoftEther VPN

In 2013 July, SoftEther VPN was released by SoftEther VPN Project with SoftEther Corporation and University of Tsukuba.

SoftEther VPN 1.0 developed based on PacketiX VPN 4.0. Compatibility and the restrictions of functions follow UT-VPN. It is scheduled to release source codes with the GNU General Public License (GPL) in 2013.[5]

On January 4, 2014, SoftEther VPN announced that the source code of SoftEther VPN was released as open-source software under the GPLv2 license. SoftEther VPN is the underlying VPN engine of VPN Gate.

27.2 External links

SoftEther Corporation

- Official website (Japanese)

- Official website (Chinese)

External Project (with University of Tsukuba)

- UT-VPN Open Source Project (Japanese)

- SoftEther VPN Project (English)

- VPN Gate Academic Experiment Project (English)

27.3 See also

- SoftEther VPN

- UT-VPN

27.4 References

[1]

[2] "PacketiX VPN 3.0 Web site". SoftEther Corporation. Retrieved 2013-08-27 (JST). Check date values in: |accessdate= (help)

[3] "PacketiX VPN 3.0 - Download". SoftEther Corporation. Retrieved 2013-08-27 (JST). Check date values in: |accessdate= (help)

[4] "New functions of PacketiX VPN 4.0 - SoftEther Web site". SoftEther Corporation. Retrieved 2013-08-27 (JST). Check date values in: |accessdate= (help)

[5] "Source Code - SoftEther VPN Project". SoftEther Project at University of Tsukuba, Japan. Retrieved 2013-08-27 (JST). Check date values in: |accessdate= (help)

Chapter 28

SoftEther VPN

SoftEther VPN is a free open-source, cross-platform, multi-protocol VPN solution developed as part of Daiyuu Nobori's master's thesis research at the University of Tsukuba. VPN protocols such as SSL VPN, L2TP/IPsec, OpenVPN and Microsoft Secure Socket Tunneling Protocol are provided in a single VPN server. It was released using the GPLv2 license on January 4, 2014.

The architecture of SoftEther VPN was designed for firewall penetration. Support for NAT traversal is provided, making it possible to set up a VPN server behind an organization's or government's firewall. Firewalls performing deep packet inspection are unable to detect SoftEther's VPN transport packets as a VPN tunnel because HTTPS is used to camouflage the connection.

Performance optimization was another objective for SoftEther VPN. It employs strategies such as full Ethernet frame utilization, reducing memory copy operations, parallel transmission, and clustering. Together, these reduce latency normally associated with VPN connections while increasing throughput.

The software includes a VPN server, VPN bridge, VPN client, VPN Server Manager for Windows, and VPN Command-Line Admin Utility.

28.1 Interoperability

The VPN Server and VPN Bridge support Windows, Linux, Mac OS (but not 10.9.x), FreeBSD and Solaris operating systems. SoftEther VPN provides its own type of VPN connection as well as interoperability with OpenVPN, Microsoft Secure Socket Tunneling Protocol (SSTP), SSL VPN, EtherIP, L2TPv3 and IPsec. Mobile devices running iOS, Android, and Windows Phone are supported via L2TP/IPsec. SoftEther's native VPN Client is supported on Windows, Linux, and Mac. VPN clients and endpoints supporting the other VPN protocols may also be used; this includes a wide variety of routers from companies such as Cisco, Juniper, Linksys (with DD-WRT), Asus, and many others.

28.2 VPN Server

SoftEther VPN Server implements the VPN server function to listens and accepts connections from VPN Client or VPN Bridge with several VPN protocols.

A VPN Server can have several Virtual Hubs and Virtual Layer-3 Switches. A Virtual Hub has full layer-2 Ethernet packet-switching functions like a physical Ethernet switch. Additionally, a Virtual Hub can be configured to define IP packet filter entries to filter the packets through the Virtual Hub. A Virtual Layer-3 Switch has layer-3 IP static routing functions like a physical router.

A VPN Server can have local-bridges. A local bridge is the layer-2 packet-switching fabric between a physical Ethernet network-adapter and a Virtual Hub. The administrator defines a local-bridge between the Virtual Hub and the existing

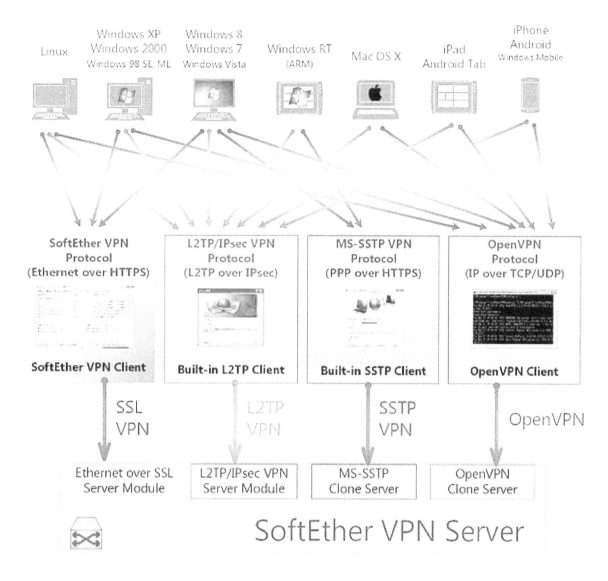

The SoftEther VPN server architecture

corporate network to build a remote-access VPN server or a site-to-site VPN server.

28.3 VPN Client

SoftEther VPN Client is a VPN client program which has the virtualized function of an Ethernet network adapter. A computer with installed SoftEther VPN Client can establish a VPN connection to the VPN Server. Since the VPN Server has the support for multiple VPN protocols such as L2TP/IPsec or MS-SSTP VPN, VPN users are not required to install SoftEther VPN Client on client computers. When a user uses L2TP/IPsec or MS-SSTP VPN to connect to the VPN Server, the built-in VPN client programs on the operating system can be used to establish a VPN to the VPN Server. However, SoftEther VPN Client has advanced functions (e.g. more detailed VPN communication settings) than OS built-in VPN clients. To exploit the full performance of SoftEther VPN Server, it is recommended to install SoftEther VPN Client on each client computer.

28.4   VPN Bridge

SoftEther VPN Bridge is a VPN program for building a site-to-site VPN. To build a site-to-site VPN network, the system administrator has to install SoftEther VPN Server on the central site, and has to install SoftEther VPN Bridge on one or more remote sites. A VPN Bridge connects to the central VPN Server by cascade connection. A cascade connection is similar to, but a virtualized of, an uplink connection (cross-cable connection) between two physical Ethernet switches.

28.5   VPN Server Manager for Windows

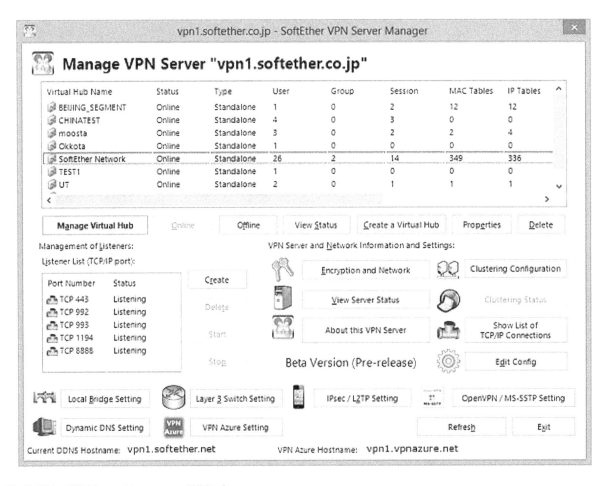

The SoftEther VPN Server Management GUI Tool

The GUI Tool is the administrative tool for SoftEther VPN Server and SoftEther VPN Bridge. It is a program that runs on both Windows and Linux with WINE. A system administrator installs the GUI Tool on his laptop PC, and makes it connect to the remote VPN Server or VPN Bridge for administration. The connection is made by SSL session, and management commands are transported as RPC over SSL.

28.6   VPN Command-Line Admin Utility

vpncmd is the CUI administrative tool for SoftEther VPN Server, Client and Bridge. It is a program that runs on consoles of every supported operating systems. When a user is unable to use Windows or Linux with WINE, the user can alternatively use vpncmd to manage the VPN programs. vpncmd is also useful to execute a batch operation, such as creating many users on the Virtual Hub, or creating many Virtual Hubs on the VPN Server.

28.7 Features[4]

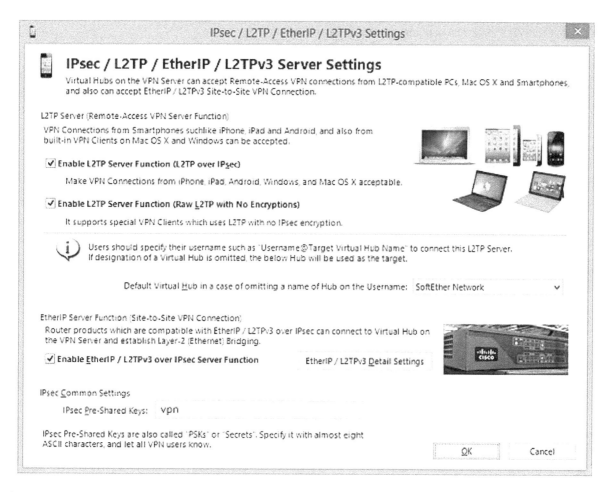

The IPsec / L2TP setting screen for iPhone and iPad

- Free and open-source software.

- Easy to establish both remote-access and site-to-site VPN.

- SSL-VPN Tunneling on HTTPS to pass through NATs and firewalls.

- Revolutionary VPN over ICMP and VPN over DNS features.

- Resistance to highly restricted firewall.

- Ethernet-bridging (L2) and IP-routing (L3) over VPN.

- Embedded dynamic-DNS and NAT-traversal so that no static nor fixed IP address is required.

- AES 256-bit and RSA 4096-bit encryptions.

- Sufficient security features such as logging and firewall inner VPN tunnel.

- 1Gbit/s-class high-speed throughput performance with low memory and CPU usage.

- Windows, Linux, Mac, Android, iPhone, iPad and Windows Phone are supported.

- SSL-VPN (HTTPS) and 6 major VPN protocols (OpenVPN, IPsec, L2TP, MS-SSTP, L2TPv3 and EtherIP) are all supported as VPN tunneling underlay protocols.

- The OpenVPN clone function supports legacy OpenVPN clients.

- IPv4 / IPv6 dual-stack.

- The VPN server runs on Windows, Linux, FreeBSD, Solaris and Mac OS X.

- Configure All settings on GUI.

- Multi-languages (English, Japanese and Simplified-Chinese).

- No memory leaks. High quality stable codes, intended for long-term runs. We always verify that there are no memory or resource leaks before releasing the build.

- RADIUS / NT Domain user authentication function

- RSA certificate authentication function

- Deep-inspect packet logging function

- Source IP address control list function

- Syslog transfer function

- SoftEther VPN is safe from the Heartbleed vulnerability of OpenSSL. (April 11, 2014)

28.8   Architecture[5]

Some parts of the architecture of SoftEther VPN are different from typical traditional IPsec-based VPN systems.

28.8.1   Full Ethernet Virtualization

The key concept of the method of realizing VPN by SoftEther VPN is the full virtualization of Ethernet segments, layer-2 Ethernet switches and Ethernet adapters.

Since SoftEther VPN tunnels the Internet and establishes a VPN Session between remote sites with full capabilities to transmit any Ethernet packets, SoftEther VPN has unlimited protocol transparency exactly the same as physical Ethernet segments. There are many protocols which can be used on Ethernet. For example, IPv4 (TCP, UDP, ICMP, ESP, GRE etc.), IPv6 (the next generation of IP), NetBEUI, IPX/SPX, PPPoE, RIP, STP and so on. All protocols can be transmitted on the tunnel by SoftEther VPN.

Legacy VPN systems with L2TP, IPsec or PPTP can transmit only IPv4, because these VPN protocols can carry only the upper layer of equal or more than layer-3. In contrast, SoftEther VPN can carry any packets which are equal or more than layer-2.

The user can derive a benefit from this advantage. The user can use any legacy and latest protocols within the VPN session of SoftEther VPN. If the user's company uses some specified protocol for controlling a manufacturing machine, the user can use it on the SoftEther VPN session. No modifications on the software are needed to use such a protocol on the layer-2 VPN.

The forwarding database (FDB) of a Virtual Hub

28.8.2   Virtual Hub

A Virtual Hub is the software-emulated virtual Ethernet switch. It learns and maintains its own forwarding-database table inside. While traditional physical Ethernet switches implement this function by hardware, SoftEther VPN implements the same function by software. A VPN Server can have several Virtual Hubs. Each Virtual Hub is isolated. A Virtual Hub performs the packet-switching between concurrently connected VPN sessions to realize the communication between VPN Clients and VPN Bridges.

When there are several Virtual Hubs in a single instance of VPN Server, these Virtual Hubs are isolated for security. Each different administrator can have the delegated privilege for each correspondent Virtual Hub. An administrator for a Virtual Hub can define user-objects and ACLs, limited only the delegated Virtual Hub.

28.8.3   Virtual Network Adapter

A Virtual Network Adapter is the software-emulated virtual Ethernet adapter. A VPN Client can create several Virtual Network Adapters on the client computer. A VPN user can establish a VPN session between the Virtual Network Adapter and the destination Virtual Hub of the remote VPN Server. While the VPN session is established, the VPN user can communicate to the remote VPN network through the Virtual Network Adapter. Since the Virtual Network Adapter works as if it were the physical one, any applications or operating system components can be used without any modification.

28.8.4   Virtual Layer-3 Switch

A Virtual Layer-3 Switch is the software-emulated virtual IP router. Several Virtual Layer-3 Switches can be created on a single VPN Server instance. A Virtual Layer-3 Switch has virtual IP interfaces connected to Virtual Hubs. It also has several static routing table entries.

The Virtual Layer-3 Switch is useful to make a large-scale site-to-site VPN network. Although the easy way to make a site-to-site VPN network is to build the layer-2 bridging based VPN, if the number of computers is huge the number of broadcasting packets will increase to load the inter-site links. To prevent that scaling problem, the VPN administrator isolates IP networks by Virtual Layer-3 switch.

28.8.5   Cascade Connection between Virtual Hubs

The administrator can define a cascade connection between local or remote Virtual Hubs. After the cascade connection has been established, the originally-isolated two Ethernet segments are combined to the single Ethernet segment. Therefore, the cascade connection function is used to build the site-to-site layer-2 Ethernet bridging.

28.8.6   Local Bridge between Virtual Hubs and Physical Ethernet Segment

Since Virtual Hubs and Virtual Network Adapters are only software-emulated virtual Ethernet devices, the Ethernet packets through these virtual devices cannot communicate with physical Ethernet devices. Therefore, a bridge between the virtual and the physical is necessary to build a remote-access VPN or site-to-site VPN. To make a bridge, the Local Bridge function exchanges the Ethernet packets between a Virtual Hub and a physical Ethernet network adapter to combine both isolated Ethernet segments into a single Ethernet segment.

After defining the Local Bridge on SoftEther VPN Server, any VPN Client can connect to the VPN Server and communicate to all existing Ethernet devices (e.g. servers or network equipment) through the Local Bridge. This is called a remote-access VPN.

If the network administrator sets up the remote-site VPN Bridge, and defines two Local Bridges on both VPN Server and VPN Bridge, and defines a cascade connection between VPN Server and VPN Bridge, then the remote two Ethernet segments are connected directly in layer-2 Ethernet level. This is called a site-to-site VPN.

28.8.7   Firewall, Proxy and NAT Transparency

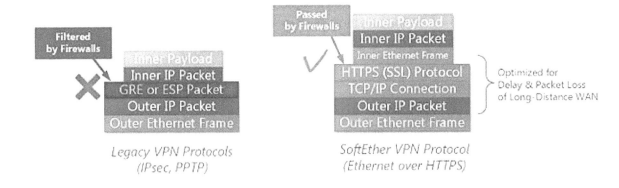

Firewall, Proxy and NAT Transparency

One of the key features of SoftEther VPN is the transparency for firewalls, proxy servers and NATs (Network Address Translators). To do this, SoftEther VPN supports SSL-VPN and NAT Traversal. SoftEther VPN uses HTTPS protocol in order to establish a VPN tunnel. HTTPS (HTTP over SSL) protocol uses the TCP/IP port 443 (may vary) as destination.

28.8.8   Parallel Transmission Mechanism of Multiple SSL-VPN Tunnels

When the user chooses SSL-VPN protocol between the VPN Client and VPN Server, SoftEther VPN Server and VPN Client use a parallel transmission mechanism to improve the throughput of the SSL-VPN tunnel. A user can set up the number of concurrent parallel transmission channels from 1 to 32. In an environment such as a slow and delaying network, this performance tuning will result in a faster throughput. When this function is enabled, the logical VPN Session will consist of several TCP (HTTPS) connections. All packets will be added to one of the appropriate TCP connections with calculations of optimizing modules. If some packet losses have been detected on a TCP connection of the logical VPN Session, then the new packet will use another healthy VPN connection. This fast-switching optimization to determine the processing TCP connection enables high throughput.

28.8.9   NAT Traversal

Traditional VPN systems require the user to ask the firewall's administrator of the company to open an endpoint (TCP or UDP port) on the firewall or NAT on the border between the company and the Internet. In order to reduce the necessity to open an endpoint on the firewall, SoftEther VPN Server has the NAT Traversal function. NAT Traversal is enabled by default. As long as it is enabled, SoftEther VPN Client computers can connect to your VPN Server behind the firewall or NAT. No special settings on the firewall or NAT are necessary.

28.8.10   VPN over ICMP, and VPN over DNS

A few very-restricted networks only permit to pass ICMP or DNS packets. On such a network, TCP or UDP are filtered. Only ICMP and DNS are permitted. In order to make it possible to establish a SoftEther VPN client-server session via such a very-restricted network, SoftEther VPN has the "VPN over ICMP" and the "VPN over DNS" function.

This function is very powerful to penetrate such a restricted firewall. All VPN packets are capsuled into ICMP or DNS packets to transmit over the firewall. The receiver-side endpoint extracts the inner packet from the capsuled packet. This is very useful for exploiting public Wi-Fi. Some public Wi-Fi can pass only ICMP or DNS packets. They filter TCP or UDP packets. If you have a VPN Server installed on your home or office in advance to go outdoor, you can enjoy protocol-free network communication by using such a restricted network.

28.8.11   VPN Gate

VPN Gate is a plugin for SoftEther VPN, which allows users to connect to free VPN servers, run by volunteers who use SoftEther to host their VPN servers. VPN Gate is sponsored by the University of Tsukuba. [6][7]

28.9   See also

- OpenVPN, an open-source VPN program

- UDP hole punching, a technique for establishing UDP "connections" between firewalled/NATed network nodes

- Secure Socket Tunneling Protocol (SSTP) Microsoft method for implementing PPP over SSL VPN

28.10   References

[1] Authors of SoftEther VPN on GitHub

[2] Multi-language, Single Binary Package and Unicode Support

[3] License of SoftEther VPN

[4] Features of SoftEther VPN

[5] Layer-2 Ethernet-based VPN

[6] http://www.vpngate.net/en/about_faq.aspx

[7] http://www.vpngate.net/en/join.aspx

28.11   External links

- SoftEther VPN Project web site

- SoftEther VPN Users Forum

- Create SoftEther VPN Account Online

- Multi-protocol SoftEther VPN becomes open source (by net-security.org)

- Multi-Protocol SoftEther VPN Becomes Open Source (by Linux Today)

Chapter 29

strongSwan

strongSwan is a complete IPsec implementation for Linux 2.6 and 3.x kernels. The focus of the project is on strong authentication mechanisms using X.509 public key certificates and optional secure storage of private keys on smartcards through a standardized PKCS#11 interface.

29.1 Overview

The project is actively maintained by Andreas Steffen who is a professor for Security in Communications at the University of Applied Sciences in Rapperswil, Switzerland.[2]

As a descendant of the FreeS/WAN project, strongSwan continues to be released under the GPL license.[3] It supports certificate revocation lists and the Online Certificate Status Protocol (OCSP). A unique feature is the use of X.509 attribute certificates to implement access control schemes based on group memberships. StrongSwan interoperates with other IPsec implementations, including various Microsoft Windows and Mac OS X VPN clients. The modular strongSwan 5.0 branch fully implements the Internet Key Exchange (IKEv2) protocol defined by RFC 5996.[4]

29.2 Features

StrongSwan supports IKEv1 and fully implements IKEv2.[4]

29.2.1 IKEv1 and IKEv2 features

- strongSwan offers plugins, enhancing its functionality. The user can choose among three crypto libraries (legacy [non-US] FreeS/WAN, OpenSSL, and gcrypt).

- Using the openssl plugin, strongSwan supports Elliptic Curve Cryptography (ECDH groups and ECDSA certificates and signatures) both for IKEv2 and IKEv1, so that interoperability with Microsoft's Suite B implementation on Vista, Win 7, Server 2008, etc. is possible.

- Automatic assignment of virtual IP addresses to VPN clients from one or several address pools using either the IKEv1 ModeConfig or IKEv2 Configuration payload. The pools are either volatile (i.e. RAM-based) or stored in a SQLite or MySQL database (with configurable lease-times).

- The *ipsec pool* command line utility allows the management of IP address pools and configuration attributes like internal DNS and NBNS servers.

29.2.2 IKEv2 only features

- The IKEv2 daemon is inherently multi-threaded (16 threads by default). It has been shown that up to 20,000 concurrent IPsec tunnels can be handled on industry-grade VPN gateways.

- The IKEv2 daemon comes with a High-Availability option based on Cluster IP where currently a cluster of two hosts does active load-sharing and each host can take over the ESP and IKEv2 states without rekeying if the other host fails.

- The following EAP authentication methods are supported: AKA and SIM including the management of multiple [U]SIM cards, MD5, MSCHAPv2, GTC, TLS, TTLS. EAP-MSCHAPv2 authentication based on user passwords and EAP-TLS with user certificates are interoperable with the Windows 7 Agile VPN Client.

- The EAP-RADIUS plugin relays EAP packets to one or multiple AAA servers (e.g. FreeRADIUS or Active Directory).

- Support of RFC 5998 EAP-Only Authentication in conjunction with strong mutual authentication methods like e.g. EAP-TLS.

- Support of RFC 4739 IKEv2 Multiple Authentication Exchanges.

- Support of the RFC 4555 Mobility and Multihoming Protocol (MOBIKE) which allows dynamic changes of the IP address and/or network interface without IKEv2 rekeying. MOBIKE is also supported by the Windows 7 Agile VPN Client.

- The strongSwan IKEv2 NetworkManager applet supports EAP, X.509 certificate and PKCS#11 smartcard based authentication. Assigned DNS servers are automatically installed and removed again in /etc/resolv.conf.

- Support of Trusted Network Connect (TNC). A strongSwan VPN client can act as a TNC client and a strongSwan VPN gateway as a Policy Enforcement Point (PEP) and optionally as a co-located TNC server. The following TCG interfaces are supported: IF-IMC 1.2, IF-IMV 1.2, IF-PEP 1.1, IF-TNCCS 1.1, IF-TNCCS 2.0 (RFC 5793 PB-TNC), IF-M 1.0 (RFC 5792 PA-TNC), and IF-MAP 2.0.

- The IKEv2 daemon has been fully ported to the Android operating system including integration into the Android VPN applet. It has also been ported to the Maemo, FreeBSD and Mac OS X operating systems.

29.3   KVM simulation environment

The focus of the strongSwan project lies on the strong Authentication by means of X.509-Certificates, as well as the optional safe storage of private key on smart cards with help of the standardized PKCS#11 interface, strongSwan certificate check lists and On-line Certificate Status Protocol (OCSP).

An important capability is the use of X.509 Certificate Attributes, which permits it to utilize complex access control mechanisms on the basis of group memberships.

strongSwan is however simple to configure and works smoothly with nearly all other IPsec implementations, in particular also with various Microsoft Windows and Mac OS X-VPN-products.

strongSwan comes with a simulation environment based on KVM. A network of eight virtual hosts allows the user to enact a multitude of site-to-site and roadwarrior VPN scenarios.

29.4   See also

- libreswan

- Openswan

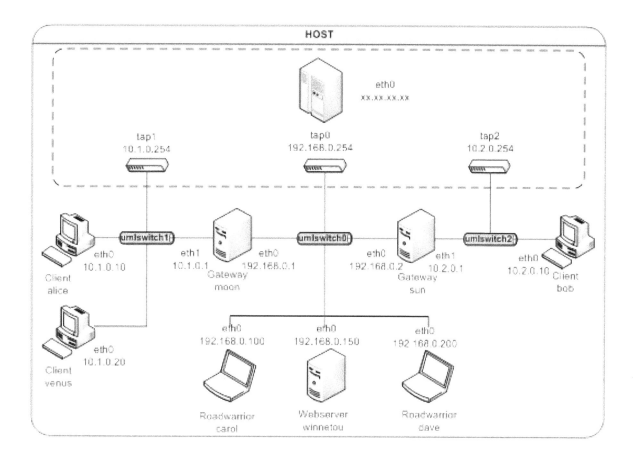

29.5   External links

- strongSwan website

- strongSwan with Trusted Network Connect (TNC)

- LinuxTag 2008 Paper: strongSwan VPNs - modularized and scalable!

- LinuxTag 2007 Paper: strongSwan - the new IKEv2 VPN Solution

- LinuxTag 2005 Paper: Advanced Features of Linux strongSwan

29.6   References

[1] strongSwan - Download

[2] "Advisors: Prof. Dr. Andreas Steffen". University of Applied Sciences. Retrieved 2015-09-28.

[3] "strongSwan - Download: License statement". 2015-09-06. Retrieved 2015-09-28.

[4] "strongSwan: the OpenSource IPsec-based VPN Solution". 2015-09-06. Retrieved 2015-09-28.

Chapter 30

Threenix

Threenix is a computer security software suite.

30.1   Overview

Threenix is a complete commercial solution for deep networking security configuration based on a pre-configured Linux platform available as both a hardware and virtual appliance. The installed software is written in Python and C++. This, communicating with core services such as *ip route* or *iptables*, provides a number of functionalities, some of which are listed below:

- Firewall

- DoS protection

- Load Balancing/Failover configuration

- Bandwidth shaping and bandwidth control

- VPN IPSEC, Open VPN and PPtP

- Antispam system

- Antivirus and Authentication

- URL filtering and Content filtering based on category database

- Spyware protection

The system displays a beautiful and simple web interface written in HTML, PHP and Javascript to help the user to enable/disable and to configure his personal services in an intuitive way. Moreover, the web interface is equipped with a remote reporter that makes easy to visualize the status of the system and the status of every single service from wherever the user may want. Threenix is released only in Italy and has been developed by **PC Service S.r.l.**. The last stable release of the platform is 4.02.00.

30.2   New version

In April 2012, PC Service S.r.l. started the development of the Threenix's new version 5, which will be completely rewritten in order to make it handle much more features and capabilities. The most important improvements will be:

- Use of a **CLI** (Common Language Interface) which will be the single point of configuration and management

- Distributed communication between components

- HA (High availability) management

As described in the following diagrams, every service can be distributed on separate appliances for maximum performance and scalability.

30.2.1 Threenix Installation Simple Block Diagram

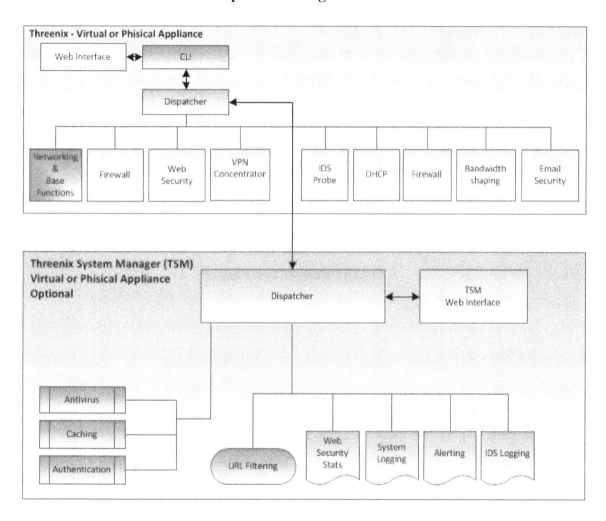

Simple Threenix Installation Block Diagram

30.2.2 Threenix Installation Complex Block Diagram

This new distribution will be available also as "Community Edition" that will be free and without support.

30.3 See also

- Application layer firewall

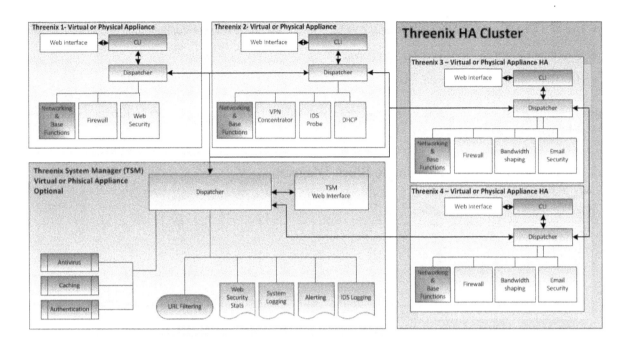

Complex Threenix Installation Block Diagram

- Comparison of firewalls
- Computer security
- Firewall
- Network security

30.4   External links

- Threenix at Sourceforge
- Threenix CLI
- Threenix Wiki
- Threenix Community Site
- Threenix Commercial Italian Site

Chapter 31

Tinc (protocol)

Tinc is a self-routing, mesh networking protocol, used for compressed, encrypted, virtual private networks. It was started in 1998 by Guus Sliepen, Ivo Timmermans, and Wessel Dankers, and released as a GPL-licensed project.

31.1 Supported network transports

- IPv4
- IPv6
- Ethernet

31.2 Embedded technologies

- OpenSSL (encryption library)
- zlib ("best compression")
- LZO ("fast compression")

31.3 Projects that use tinc

- Freifunk: tinc was enabled in their routers as of October 2006 .
- OpenWrt has an installable package for tinc.
- pfSense has an installable package in the 2.2 release
- Tomato has tinc support included in the Shibby mod.

31.4 External links

- Homepage
- Debian GNU/Linux tinc dhcp bridging setup
- "Quick & Dirty TINC setup"

79

- Gentoo Linux tinc setup

Chapter 32

TunnelBear

TunnelBear (also known as the **TunnelBear VPN**) is a virtual private network (VPN) developed by TunnelBear Inc. TunnelBear is currently available on Android, Microsoft Windows, Mac OS X and iOS. There is also a Google Chrome extension.[1] TunnelBear, similar to other VPNs, has the ability to bypass content blocking in most countries.[2] Tunnel-Bear includes 15 different countries the user can appear in; including Ireland, America, Sweden and Italy. There is also the ability to connect to the closest "tunnel". The desktop client uses AES-256 encryption while the extension uses AES 128-bit encryption.[3] When connected, the users real IP address will not be visible to the websites visited.[4]

Connection secure!
You are now browsing in private from
the United States

The pop-up that comes up when the user connects securely

32.1 See also

- Avast! SecureLine VPN

- TOR (anonymity network)

32.2 References

[1] Paul, Ian (19 May 2015). "How to easily secure your web browsing with TunnelBear's free Chrome extension". PC World. Retrieved 20 June 2015.

[2] Klosowski, Thorin (1 June 2015). "Streaming Content From Overseas: The Complete Lifehacker Guide". Lifehacker. Retrieved 20 June 2015.

[3] Sawers, Paul (12 May 2015). "Meet TunnelBear, the gorgeous VPN app that wants to bring online privacy to everyone". VentureBeat. Retrieved 20 June 2015.

[4] Boxall, Andy (13 May 2015). "Watch U.S. Netflix anywhere with TunnelBear, now available as a Chrome extension". Digital Trends. Retrieved 20 June 2015.

Chapter 33

Virtual file server

In computing, a **virtual file server** is a system consisting of one of more virtualized devices that store computer files such as documents, sound files, photographs, movies, images or databases. The server can be accessed by workstations or application servers through the **Virtual Fileserver Network** (VFN).[1][2]

The term "server" highlights the role of the virtual machine in the client-server scheme, where the clients are the applications accessing the storage. The file server usually does not run application programs on behalf of the clients. It enables storage and retrieval of data, where the computation is provided by the client. With a storage area network (SAN), the server(s) act purely as virtual storage devices, with a client maintaining the file system. With network-attached storage (NAS), the server(s) manage the file system. Both SAN and NAS servers may be virtualized so the users do not have to know which physical devices is hosting the files.[3] A virtual file server typically combines the security of virtual private networks (VPN) with file synchronization, distribution and sharing services of network file servers.[4]

Various companies offer software for use by an organization in managing virtual file servers. The operating system may be stripped-down, concerned only with file management functions such as synchronizing redundant copies of the file, failure recovery, handling concurrent updates from different clients and enforcing client access rights.[5] Some companies offer virtual file servers as a service to organizations that prefer to outsource server operations, with the servers residing in the "cloud".[6][7]

33.1 See also

- Storage virtualization
- Storage area network
- Network-attached storage
- Virtual private network
- Platform as a service

33.2 References

[1] Gilbert Held (1989). *Data and computer communications: terms, definitions, and abbreviations.* Wiley. p. 236. ISBN 0-471-92066-5.

[2] Chris Wolf (2005). *The Definitive Guide to Building Highly Scalable Enterprise File Serving Solutions.* Realtimepublishers. p. 57ff. ISBN 1-931491-47-X.

[3] "NAS virtualization explained". TechTarget. 31 Jul 2008. Retrieved 2009-09-29.

[4] Harry Singh (1996). *Heterogeneous internetworking: networking technically diverse operating systems*. Prentice Hall PTR. p. 259. ISBN 0-13-255696-0.

[5] Lillian N. Cassel, Richard H. Austing (2000). *Computer Networks and open systems: an application development perspective*. Jones & Bartlett Publishers. p. 209ff. ISBN 0-7637-1122-5.

[6] Schofield, Jack (17 April 2008). "Google angles for business users with 'platform as a service'". London: Guardian (UK). Retrieved 2009-09-29.

[7] "Comparing Amazon's and Google's Platform-as-a-Service (PaaS) Offerings". zdnet. April 11, 2008. Retrieved 2009-09-29.

Chapter 34

VNS3

VNS3 is a hybrid overlay networking appliance for cloud computing and virtual networks.[3] VNS3 is a software-based virtual router, switch, firewall, protocol re-distributor, and SSL/IPSec VPN concentrator.[4] The Network Virtualization Software creates a customer controlled overlay network over top of the underlying network backbone [4]

34.1 Uses

Cloud users looking to eliminate cloud networking risk in public, private, or hybrid clouds use VNS3.[4] VNS3 prevents vendor lock-in and allows for high availability, geographic distribution, and cloud federation.[5] VNS3 lets enterprise datacenter administrators "create encrypted LAN between virtual machines in a private cloud, as well as encrypted WAN across multiple public clouds."[6] A quoted VNS3 customer uses VNS3 to direct and manage IPsec traffic with insight and control to comply with financial services compliance regulations.[7]

34.2 History

Developers CohesiveFT first named their multi-sourced infrastructure concept "v-cube-v." The software ran in internal production starting in 2007.[8] The company named the early commercial version of VNS3 "VPN3" or "VPN-Cubed"[6][9] and later renamed the software to VNS3 in 2012.[10] Amazon Web Services users first began downloading VPN-Cubed from the partner directory on 5 December 2008.[11] VNS3 gained popularity (as VPN-Cubed) as part of the Amazon Web Services public cloud ecosystem[12] and with independent reviews from ZDNet,[13] High Scalability,[14] InfoQ,[15] Chris Hoff,[16] and CloudAve.[17] In 2012, developers CohesiveFT released a major version update. The release updated the software to 3.0 and rebranded it as VNS3 (VNS-Cubed).[18] 451 Research analyst William Fellows wrote "VNS[3] is not only for VPNs – hence the name change – since overlays can be within a cloud, between clouds, between a private datacenter and a cloud (or clouds), or between multiple datacenters."[19] In 2013, the CohesiveFT development team released the 3.0.1 version of the product, as well as a free edition of VNS3 in Amazon Web Services.[20] VNS3 was recognized in the 6th Annual International Datacenters Awards as the winner of the Public Cloud Services & Infrastructure award[21] and a VNS3 public cloud project with the UK's Energy Savings Trust was named Runner Up for Public Sector Cloud Project of the Year in the Datacentre Solution Awards.[22] Later in 2013, the development team released a VNS3 version aimed at Cloud Service Providers (CSPs), offering VPN services as part of a cloud infrastructure solution.[23] Also in 2013, CohesiveFT joined industry group the Open Data Center Alliance.[24] In early 2014 VNS3 3.5 was released with major software updates and a new integration with Docker[25] Docker's a open source virtualization platform added the ability to run other networking applications as containers inside VNS3 virtual machines. Users can create an overlay network "as a substrate for layer 4-7 network application services – things like proxy, reverse proxy, SSL termination, content caching and network intrusion detection" William Fellows writes.[26] Since 2008, VNS3 has become available in more public cloud providers and geographic regions, including Amazon Web Services EC2,[27] GoGrid,[28] Flexiant,[29] IBM,[5] Google Compute Engine,[30] HP Cloud Services,[31] and Abiquo.[32]

34.3   Software

VNS3 software creates IPSec tunneling connections similar to a site to site VPN. The connections can ensure a single LAN connection between virtual or cloud environments[33] VNS3 gives secure access to cloud assets, extends the Virtual LAN segmentation, isolation, and security of a cloud provider's network.[16] The first VNS3 was built on a customized Ubuntu-based Linux using open source networking applications Openswan and OpenVPN.[8] The development team chose OpenVPN "primarily because it uses standard OpenSSL encryption, runs on multiple operating systems and does not require kernel patching or additional modules."[8]

VNS3 Managers are virtual machines that act as a VPN gateway for the other virtual machines in the same cloud infrastructure. VNS3 synchronizes between cloud managers using RabbitMQ.[34] VNS3 enables users to turn multicast on and off in order to work on public clouds, allowing software configurations dependent on multicast to function in the cloud.[34]

VNS3 software creates IPSec tunneling connections similar to a site-to-site VPN. The connections can ensure a single LAN network between multiple cloud environments.[35] VNS3 secures connections to cloud deployments, extends the Virtual LAN segmentation, and ensures network isolation and security in a cloud provider's virtual environment.[16]

VNS3 has a web-based UI and traditional Linux system command line interface. The VNS3 API uses a Ruby script and Ruby language binding.[36]

The developers earned a patent on the underlying cloud VPN technologies in 2010.[37]

34.4   Availability

VPN-Cubed has been available in Amazon Web Services cloud since December 5, 2008[38]

According to the CohesiveFT website, VNS3 is delivered as a virtual machine and is available in public clouds including: Amazon Web Services,[39] HP Cloud Services,[40] Google Compute Engine, ElasticHosts, IBM[5] Softlayer, Flexiant, Interoute, and Greenqloud. Private clouds availability includes: Abiquo, Eucalyptus, Openstack; and virtual infrastructures such as: Xen, VMware, KVM, Citrix.

34.4.1   Pricing

Since October 2008, VNS3 has been available for free on Amazon Web Services[41] with additional paid editions are listed on the CohesiveFT website.

34.4.2   Release History

34.5   References

[1] "VNS3 Product Release Notes".

[2] "CohesiveFT Unveils VNS3 3.5 with Docker Technology For The Co-Creation of Customizable, Flexible Cloud Network Platforms". VMblog. 30 January 2014. Retrieved 6 April 2014.

[3] "VNS3 CrunchBase Profile". CrunchBase. 14 January 2014. Retrieved 6 April 2014.

[4] contentRoy Chua (2014). "CohesiveFT VNS3". SDNCentral LLC. Retrieved 6 April 2014.

[5] "VNS3 Datacenter Connect 3.0". IBM. 25 July 2013. Retrieved 6 April 2014.

[6] Karin Kelley (29 October 2008). "CohesiveFT releases cloud security service VPN-Cubed". 451 Research. Retrieved 6 April 2014.

[7] Alan R. Earls (19 March 2014). "Stampede to cloud presents data integration problems". Techtarget. Retrieved 6 April 2014.

[8] Dmitriy Samovskiy (1 February 2008). "Building a Multisourced Infrastructure Using OpenVPN". Linux Journal. Retrieved 20 November 2013.

[9] Dmitriy Samovskiy (2008-03-12). "VcubeV". Dmitriy Samovskiy. Retrieved 10 December 2010.

[10] "VNS3 Release Notes". CohesiveFT. Retrieved 10 December 2013.

[11] "VPN-Cubed". Amazon Web Services. 5 December 2008. Retrieved 6 April 2014.

[12] Jeff Barr (31 October 2008). "New and Cool - VPN-Cubed & Glue". Amazon Web Services Blog. Retrieved 10 December 2013.

[13] Phil Wainewright (19 February 2008). "How to deploy to the cloud of your choice". ZDnet. Retrieved 6 April 2014.

[14] Todd Hoff (4 March 2008). "Manage Downtime Risk By Connecting Multiple Data Centers Into A Secure Virtual LAN". High Scalability. Retrieved 6 April 2014.

[15] Jean-Jacques Dubray (28 October 2008). "A VPN for Cloud Computing". InfoQ. Retrieved 6 April 2014.

[16] Christopher Hoff (2008-11-14). "CohesiveFT VPN-Cubed: Not Your Daddy's Encrypted Tunnel". Rational Security. Retrieved 10 December 2013.

[17] Krishnan Subramanian (28 October 2008). "VPN Cubed – Cloud is Ready for the Enterprise". CloudAve. Retrieved 6 April 2014.

[18] "VNS3 Release Notes". CohesiveFT. Retrieved 6 April 2014.

[19] William Fellows (29 May 2013). "Extending into the cloud: CohesiveFT redefined for its VNS network software". 451 Research. Retrieved 6 April 2014.

[20] "CohesiveFT Announces Free Trial Edition for VNS3, Technical Update". Wall Street Journal. 17 April 2013. Retrieved 6 April 2014.

[21] "International Datacentre and Cloud Awards Announced for 2013". Broad Group. 7 January 2013. Retrieved 6 April 2014.

[22] "IAnd the winners are.". DSC Europe. 29 May 2013. Retrieved 6 April 2014.

[23] Paula Bernier (9 October 2013). "CohesiveFT: SDN, NFV Can Enable CSP Differentiation with VPCs". SDN Zone. Retrieved 6 April 2014.

[24] "CohesiveFT Joins Open Data Center Alliance". Hosting News. 13 March 2013. Retrieved 6 April 2014.

[25] "CohesiveFT Unveils VNS3 3.5 with Docker Technology For The Co-Creation of Customizable, Flexible Cloud Network Platforms". VMblog. 30 January 2014. Retrieved 6 April 2014.

[26] William Fellows (27 February 2014). "CohesiveFT ships Docker with latest network overlay release". [451 Research]. Retrieved 6 April 2014.

[27] Robin Wauters (4 March 2009). "CohesiveFT Releases VPN-Cubed for EC2". Virtualization.com. Retrieved 6 April 2014.

[28] Jason Verge (8 January 2010). "GoGrid partners: typical cloud pieces being addressed through tech partnerships". 451 Research. Retrieved 6 April 2014.

[29] "Flexiant and CohesiveFT Join Forces to Offer Virtual Private Clouds On Extility". Flexiant. 23 June 2010. Retrieved 6 April 2014.

[30] "CohesiveFT Joins Google Cloud Platform Partner Program". Reuters. 5 November 2013. Retrieved 6 April 2014.

[31] "CohesiveFT Offers Customers Secure and Flexible Networking Features in the HP Public Cloud". Yahoo Finance. 12 Nov 2013. Retrieved 6 April 2014.

[32] "Abiquo and CohesiveFT Offer Software Defined Networking to Expand Cloud Platform's Flexibility and Security". Abiquo. 4 December 2013. Retrieved 6 April 2014.

[33] Krishnan Narayan (2013-07-02). "Smart gateway for AWS Virtual Private Clouds". Symantec. Retrieved 2013-11-20.

[34] William Fellows (17 November 2008). "CohesiveFT's VPN-Cubed offers some cloud control". 451 Research. Retrieved 6 April 2014.

[35] Krishnan Narayan (2 July 2013). "Smart gateway for AWS Virtual Private Clouds". Symantec. Retrieved 20 November 2013.

[36] Patrick Kerpan (17 November 2010). "API Tools and Documentation" (PDF). CohesiveFT. Retrieved 10 December 2013.

[37] *US 20100115606 A1*, Google Patents, retrieved 10 December 2013

[38] "Customer Apps: VPN-Cubed". Amazon Web Services. 5 December 2008. Retrieved 10 December 2013.

[39] "VNS3 Free Edition". Amazon Web Services. Retrieved 10 December 2013.

[40] "CohesiveFT VNS3". HP Cloud Services. Retrieved 10 December 2013.

[41] Krishnan Subramanian (2009-03-04). "VPNCubed Available For EC2 Including A Free Version". Cloud Ave. Retrieved 10 December 2013.

[42] "VNS3 Release Notes". CohesiveFT. Retrieved 9 December 2013.

[43] "New CohesiveFT VNS3 Cloud Service Provider Edition Increases Revenue Generating Opportunities". Yahoo Finance. 20 August 2013. Retrieved 6 April 2014.

[44] "VNS Provider Edition". CohesiveFT. Retrieved 6 April 2014.

34.6 External links

- Official website

- Network World Products of the Week featuring VNS3

- Open Data Center Alliance member page, featuring VNS3

Chapter 35

VPN blocking

VPN blocking is a technique used to block the encrypted protocol tunneling communications methods used by virtual private network (VPN) systems. Often used by large organizations such as national governments or corporations, it can act as a tool for computer security or Internet censorship by preventing the use of VPNs to bypass network firewall systems.

35.1 Description

Blocking VPN access can be done a few different ways. Ports that are used by common VPN tunneling protocols, such as PPTP or L2TP, to establish their connections and transfer data can be closed by system administrators to prevent their use on certain networks. Similarly, a website can prohibit access to its content by blocking access from IP addresses that are known to belong to popular VPN providers. Some governments have been known to block all access to overseas IP addresses, since VPN use often entails connecting to remote hosts that do not operate under that government's jurisdiction.[1]

As organizations have ramped up efforts to block VPN access bypassing their firewalls, VPN providers have responded by utilizing more sophisticated techniques to make their connections less conspicuous, creating a networking arms race. For instance, as the Chinese government began using deep packet inspection to identify VPN protocols, Golden Frog began scrambling OpenVPN packet metadata for its popular VyprVPN service in an attempt to avoid detection.[2]

35.2 Government use

35.2.1 China

See also: Golden Shield Project

Chinese internet users started reporting unstable connections in May 2011 while using VPNs to connect to overseas websites and services such as the Apple App Store.[3] Universities and businesses began issuing notices to stop using tools to circumvent the firewall.

In late 2012, companies providing VPN services claimed the Great Firewall of China became able to "learn, discover and block" the encrypted communications methods used by a number of different VPN systems. China Unicom, one of the biggest telecoms providers in the country, is now blocking connections where a VPN is detected, according to one company with a number of users in China.[4]

In early 2015, China cracked down on VPNs, software that allows internet users to access Twitter, Facebook, Gmail and others websites blocked in the country, according to state media and service providers. Many users reported VPN service disruptions. However, some VPN providers still work in China.[5]

35.2.2 Iran

See also: Internet censorship in Iran

The government of Iran began blocking access to non-government sanctioned VPNs in March 2013,[6] a few months prior to the 2013 elections, to "prosecute users who are violating state laws" and "take offenders to national courts under supervision of judiciary service". Use of VPNs approved by the government reportedly led to surveillance and inspection of private data.[7]

35.3 VPN blocking by online services

35.3.1 Hulu

In an attempt to combat piracy from unauthorized users outside the US, Hulu began blocking users accessing the site from IP addresses linked to VPN services in April 2014. In doing so, however, the company also restricted access from legitimate U.S.-based users using VPNs for security reasons. VPN providers such as VikingVPN and TorGuard stated that they would seek ways to address this issue for their customers by speaking directly to Hulu about a resolution and rolling out more dedicated IP addresses, respectively.[8]

35.3.2 Netflix

Netflix came under pressure from major film studios in September 2014 to block VPN access, as up to 200,000 Australian subscribers were using Netflix despite it not being available yet in Australia.[9] VPN access for Netflix has, like other streaming services, allowed users to view content more securely or while out of the country. Netflix users have also used VPNs as a means of bypassing throttling efforts made by service providers such as Verizon.[10]

35.4 References

[1] Lam, Oiwan. "China: Cracking down circumvention tools".

[2] Toombs, Zach. "China's Censors Take on Virtual Private Networks". Retrieved 13 November 2014.

[3] Arthur, Charles. "China cracks down on VPN use".

[4] Arthur, Charles (14 December 2012). "China tightens 'Great Firewall' internet control with new technology". *guardian.co.uk*. The Guardian. Retrieved 2013-06-11.

[5] "China VPN". *BestVPNProvider.com*. Retrieved 7 May 2015.

[6] Torbati, Yeganeh. "Iran blocks use of tool to get around Internet filter".

[7] Shwayder, Maya. "Cyber-Rebels See Way To Get Around Iran's VPN Internet Block".

[8] Van Der Sar, Ernesto. "Hulu Blocks VPN Users Over Piracy Concerns".

[9] Maxwell, Andy. "VPN Users 'Pirating' Netflix Scare TV Networks".

[10] Nederkoorn, Colin. "Verizon made an enemy tonight".

35.5 See also

- Deep packet inspection
- Steganographic tunnel

Chapter 36

Dacloud.me

Dacloud.me is a virtual private network service that uses encrypted connection to mask original IP addresses during online surfing and peer to peer sharing. The company is very known in Europe, Middle East and Northern America for its strict privacy policy and quality of service.

Dacloud.me provides relatively better support, faster performance, and high compatibility due to its proprietary technologies on top of the already existing Open Source OpenVPN Project. This ensures that the core functionalities of the platform remain untouched without compromising the need of new innovative features.

The service requires relatively small open VPN software to run, like OpenVPN. There is minimal variety of geographic locations. Available servers include the United States, France, Germany, Singapore, United Kingdom and Netherlands.[1] Dacloud.me is often used to bypass some network restrictions, ISP's throttling, or geographical limitations. It can also protect against Computer Hackers and Traffic Sniffers.

36.1 Installation

The client is distributed with an executable installer for Windows, Max OS X, iOS, Android and Linux operating systems. The profile files are available on Dacloud.me Pannels to login to a VPN client via the server pannel. For iPad and Android operating system OpenVPN Connect application can be downloaded from Apple App Store and Google Play store. Unzip the certificate bundles and can be connected to Dacloud.me server through server profile information contained within the file itself.

36.2 Platform

The software is installed on a separate operating system, which provides the protocol stack, file system, process scheduling and other features needed to deliver the maximum security. Dacloud.me's Windows Client is already available for download on the official website or on major software sites like CNET.

36.3 References

[1] *""* *Dacloud.me*

36.4 External links

- Official website

36.5   See also

- BartVPN

- OpenVPN

Chapter 37

VPNBook

VPNBook is a virtual private network service that uses encrypted connection to mask original IP addresses during online surfing and peer to peer sharing.[1] ZeroPaid listed it as Number 1 on its list of Top Five Free VPN Services,[2] and on the PC Magazine review VPNBook received four out of five stars and it was depicted as having "decent performance".[3]

The service requires an OpenVPN client or means to establish a PPTP connection to be used. There are minimal variety of geographic locations. Available servers include the United States, Canada and Romania.[4] VPNBook is often used to bypass some governmental restrictions.[5][6]

37.1 Usage

The services offers two means of usage, connection via a third-party OpenVPN client or through PPTP. Any operating system that support PPTP connections can utilize VPNBook's service. The profile files for OpenVPN clients are available on VPNBook's website. The Mac OS X[7] iOS,[8] Android,[9] Ubuntu,[10] and Windows[11] operating systems all have PPTP support built in.

37.2 Platform

The software (OpenVPN clients) is installed on a separate operating system, which provides the protocol stack, file system, process scheduling and other features needed by the product.[12] However, any device that can establish a PPTP connection can utilize VPNBook. A variety of OpenVPN client are available on Windows 7, 8, XP, Mac OS X, Ubuntu, iOS and Android.

37.3 References

[1] "7 способов зайти на заблокированные сайты с ПК, смартфона и планшета". Retrieved 15 March 2014.

[2] "Top 5 Free VPN Services" *ZeroPaid.com*

[3] "VPNBook", a PC Magazine review.

[4] "Free VPN" *VPNBook.com*

[5] "Free OpenVPN Account" *VPNBook.com*

[6] Young Yang. *100+ Free Tools For You To Access Blocked Sites*. ISBN 1623145856.

[7] "OS X Mountain Lion: Set up a connection to a virtual private network" *Apple.com*

[8] "iOS: Setting up VPN" *Apple.com*

[9] "Connect to a PPTP VPN from your Andriod Phone" *TechRepublic.com*

[10] "VPNClient" *Ubuntu.com*

[11] "How to Set Up a VPN in Windows 7" *PCWorld.com*

[12] Junaid Ahmad (August 15, 2013). "How to Setup VPN in Windows 7 using VpnBook". Hackstoday. Retrieved 15 March 2014.

37.4   External links

- Official website

- VPNBook review at PC Magazine

37.5   See also

- PPTP

- OpenVPN

Chapter 38

Vyatta

Vyatta provides software-based virtual router, virtual firewall and VPN products for Internet Protocol networks (IPv4 and IPv6). A free download of Vyatta has been available since March 2006. The system is a specialized Debian-based Linux distribution with networking applications such as Quagga, OpenVPN, and many others. A standardized management console, similar to Juniper JUNOS or Cisco IOS, in addition to a web-based GUI and traditional Linux system commands, provides configuration of the system and applications. In recent versions of Vyatta, web-based management interface is supplied only in the subscription edition. However, all functionality is available through KVM, serial console or SSH/telnet protocols. The software runs on standard x86-64 servers.

Vyatta is also delivered as a virtual machine file and can provide (vrouter, vfirewall, VPN) functionality for Xen, VMware, KVM, Rackspace[1] and Amazon EC2 virtual and cloud computing environments. As of October, 2012, Vyatta has also been available through Amazon Marketplace and can be purchased as a service to provide VPN, cloud bridging and other network functions to users of Amazon's AWS services.

Vyatta sells a subscription edition that includes all the functionality of the open source version as well as a graphical user interface, access to Vyatta's RESTful API's, Serial Support, TACACS+, Config Sync, System Image Cloning, software updates, 24x7 phone and email technical support, and training. Certification as a Vyatta Professional is now available. Vyatta also offers professional services and consulting engagements.

The Vyatta system is intended as a replacement for Cisco IOS 1800 through ASR 1000[2] series Integrated Services Routers (ISR) and ASA 5500 security appliances, with a strong emphasis on the cost and flexibility inherent in an open source, Linux-based system[3] running on commodity x86 hardware or in VMware ESXi, Microsoft Hyper-V, Citrix XenServer, Open Source Xen and KVM virtual environments.

In 2012, Brocade Communications Systems acquired Vyatta and renamed it "Vyatta, a Brocade Company". In April, 2013, Brocade renamed the product from the Vyatta Subscription Edition (VSE) to the Brocade Vyatta 5400 vRouter.[4] The latest commercial release of the Brocade vRouter is no longer open-source based.

38.1   Vyatta Core

The free community Vyatta Core software (VC) is an open source network operating system providing advanced IPv4 and IPv6 routing, stateful firewalling, secure communication through both an IPSec based VPN as well as through the SSL based OpenVPN.[5]

In October 2013 an independent group started a fork of Vyatta Core under the name VyOS.[6]

38.1.1   Release History

38.2   References

[1] "Rackspace Cloud Servers Brocade Vyatta vRouter". Rackspace. Retrieved 2014-11-02.

[2] Larry Chaffin (2010-01-17). "Putting Realism Into Your Network: 10Gbps Routing + Security for under $5k, and it's not from Cisco or Juniper". Network World. Retrieved 2012-01-28.

[3] Kelly Herrell (2009-12-18). "Intel Takes Vyatta to 10Gig". Retrieved 2012-01-28.

[4] http://newsroom.brocade.com/press-releases/brocade-unites-physical-and-virtual-networking-to--nasdaq-brcd-1011704

[5] See http://www.vyatta.org

[6] vyos.net

[7] http://www.vyatta.com/downloads/documentation/VC6.6/VyattaRN_6.6R1_v01.pdf

[8] http://vyatta.org/node/14232 http://vyatta.org/node/14232

[9] "Vyatta Roadmap". Vyatta.org. Retrieved 2012-06-12.

[10] "Press Releases". www.vyatta.com. Retrieved 2012-06-12.

[11] tmccafferty (2010-03-30). "View topic - Vyatta Version 6.0 is here!". Vyatta.org. Retrieved 2012-06-12.

[12] Subscription versions now are different from core only with additional components, other features are the same.

[13] "View topic - VC5 Released". Vyatta.org. Retrieved 2012-06-12.

[14] "View topic - About branch hollister". Vyatta.org. 2008-04-30. Retrieved 2012-06-12.

[15] "View topic - VC4.1 (Hollywood) released to stable". Vyatta.org. Retrieved 2012-06-12.

[16] DaveRoberts (2008-04-21). "View topic - VC4 released". Vyatta.org. Retrieved 2012-06-12.

[17] "Bug 2544 – Glendale's Nightly-built Version Should be Changed to glendale (instead of eureka beta)". Bugzilla.vyatta.com. Retrieved 2012-06-12.

[18] "Vyatta Community Edition 3 - Routing,Firewall,VPN enhancements". ItsyourIP.com. Retrieved 2012-06-12.

[19] "Press Releases". www.vyatta.com. Retrieved 2012-06-12.

[20] "[Vyatta-users] ANN: Glendale timeline". Mail-archive.com. 2008-01-14. Retrieved 2012-06-12.

[21]

38.3   External links

- Official website
- Open Source Community

Chapter 39

VyOS

VyOS is a fork of the now defunct Vyatta Core edition of routing software. VyOS is a Linux based routing solution built on the Debian Linux distribution, and currently runs on x86 and x86-64 platforms.[1]

VyOS provides a free and open source routing platform that competes directly with other commercially available solutions from well known network providers. Because VyOS runs on standard x86 systems, it is able to be used as a router and firewall platform for cloud deployments.[2]

39.1   History

After Brocade Communications stopped development of the Vyatta Core Edition of the Vyatta Routing software, a small group of enthusiasts took the last Community Edition, and worked on building an Open Source fork to live on in place of the end of life VC.[3][4]

39.2   Releases

VyOS version 1.0.0 (Hydrogen)[5] was released on December 22, 2013, approximately one year later on December, 9 2014 version 1.1.0 (Helium) was released.[6] All versions released thus far have been based on Debian 6.0 (Squeeze), and are available as a 32-bit images and 64-bit images for both physical and virtual machines.[6]

Keeping with the naming convention the next release will be Lithium.

39.2.1   Release History

39.2.2   VMware Support

With the February 3rd 2014 maintenance release, there was the release of the VyOS OVA image for VMware. This allows for a convenient setup of VyOS on a VMware platform, and includes all of the VMware tools installed. The OVA image can be downloaded from the standard download sites, or can be downloaded from VMware.[7]

39.2.3   Amazon EC2 Support

Starting with version 1.0.2 there is the ability for Amazon EC2 customers to select an AMI image of the VyOS software.[8]

39.3   List of router or Firewall Software

List of router or firewall distributions

39.4   External links

- Distrowatch page

- Official website

- Download Mirror

- VyOS on GitHub

39.5   References

[1] "VyOS home page". Retrieved 2014-11-09.

[2] "VyOS on DistroWatch.com". Retrieved 2014-11-09.

[3] http://de.reddit.com/r/networking/comments/1o7n16/vyatta_now_rehosted_to_github_as_vyos/

[4] http://www.reddit.com/r/networking/comments/1thfaw/release_vyos_100_an_enhanced_fork_based_from_the/

[5] http://vyos.net/wiki/Hydrogen

[6] "VyOS - 1.0.0 release".

[7] "VMWare - VyOS". Retrieved 2014-11-09.

[8] "VyOS on AWS Marketplace". Retrieved 2014-11-09.

Chapter 40

WinGate

WinGate is integrated multi-protocol proxy server, email server and internet gateway from Qbik New Zealand Limited in Auckland. It was first released in October 1995, and began as a re-write of SocketSet, a product that had been previously released in prototype form by Adrien de Croy.

WinGate proved popular, and by the mid to late 1990s, WinGate was used in homes and small businesses that needed to share a single Internet connection between multiple networked computers. The introduction of Internet Connection Sharing in Windows 98, combined with increasing availability of cheap NAT-enabled routers, forced WinGate to evolve to provide more than just internet connection sharing features. Today, focus for WinGate is primarily access control, email server, caching, reporting, bandwidth management and content filtering.

WinGate comes in three versions, Standard, Professional and Enterprise. The Enterprise edition also provides an easily configured virtual private network system, which is also available separately as WinGate VPN. Licensing is based on the number of concurrently connected users, and a range of license sizes are available. Multiple licenses can also be aggregated.

The current version of WinGate is version 8.5.2 released in October 2015.[1]

40.1 Free version

From WinGate 1.0 through to WinGate 4.5.3, WinGate could be used without payment in a 1 + 1 configuration (1 on the proxy computer, one on the LAN). This free version was discontinued with WinGate 5.0.

A free license was re-introduced with the release of WinGate 7.2, and enables 3 LAN users free access, with the features associated with a WinGate Standard level license. Users choose a free license option when activating the product.

40.2 Platforms

From version 6.5 onwards, WinGate runs on Microsoft Windows from Windows 2000 (*) to Windows 10, both 32 and 64 bit. Prior versions are still available for earlier OSes back to Microsoft Windows 95.

(*) With the release of WinGate 8.0 in 2013, support for Windows 2000 was dropped.

40.3 Features

At its core, WinGate provides 3 levels of Internet Access: a stateful packet-level firewall with NAT, several circuit-level proxies (SOCKS 4/4a/5, and proprietary Winsock redirector), and multiple application-level proxy servers. This provides a comprehensive access framework, and allows the maximum level of access control.

WinGate's policy framework allows the creation of specific access rules, based on user account details, request details, location of user, authentication and time of day. Security is based on user authentication. WinGate allows use of either WinGate's built-in user database, the Windows user database, or the user database of an NT domain or Active Directory. Authentication can use integrated windows usernames and passwords (NTLM) and other authentication schemes. WinGate can also be used without authentication, or can assume user identity based on IP address or computer name.

WinGate can also authenticate individual users on a terminal server, and maintain separate user contexts to provide user-level control, and for applications that do not support authentication by using the WinGate Client software.

WinGate provides a fully customizable, self-configuring DHCP server to assist with network configuration. It also supports multi-interface and multiple topology deployment including multiple DMZs.

WinGate provides an integrated Email server (POP3 server and retrieval client, SMTP server, and IMAP4 server) with message routing features and per-email restrictions. This can be used to provide company email services, or to provide protection and additional security (encryption and authentication) for an existing email system.

The WWW Proxy provides a transparent proxy for ease of administration, plus a shared proxy cache for improved surfing performance. It can also be used to secure access to internal web servers (Reverse proxy).

Proxy services in WinGate support SSL/TLS connections, dynamic network binding (automatic response to network events such as addition or removal of network interfaces), and gateway pre-selection (to direct service for a particular application out a specific Internet connection).

Packet-level bandwidth management is also provided to allow control of bandwidth associated with certain users or applications, and is able to be configured on a per-time-of-day basis.

Also available for WinGate are optional components that provide Antivirus scanning for email, web and FTP, and content filtering for web traffic.

40.4   Other features

WinGate 7 included a number of other features. Since it is based on a generic event processing system, with pluggable event sources, and event processors, it is capable of many other applications. Also the notification system in WinGate 7 allows for definition of notification escalation plans and responses to detected events.

This opened WinGate up to being a generic monitoring and alerting system, able to monitor system metrics, check thresholds and issue notifications.

The events relating to email also permit WinGate 7 to be used as a general purpose mail processor.

40.5   Early history

The company Qbik was formed in December 1995 to monetize the first for-payment version of the software which was version 1.2 (prior versions had been free). WinGate was a text-book example of near exponential growth in product popularity due to the enormous growth in Internet usage that was occurring world-wide in the mid-1990s. A feature of this was month-on-month compound growth in excess of 20% for a sustained period (several years). As demand and workload grew so quickly, Adrien de Croy turned initially to several friends to provide additional capacity, including Tim Warren (a friend from the Auckland Youth Orchestra), and Lyle Bainbridge (who started working on WinGate code with version 1.3 in early 1996). Distribution also grew as demand for WinGate caused many software distributors and resellers to take up WinGate. In 1997, Deerfield Communications Inc was appointed sole distributor world-wide. This relationship ended in 2003, with Qbik resuming distribution and support. It is commonly thought that Deerfield owned WinGate, but this was never the case.

Other key points in early history were various OEM arrangements with companies like Compaq, 3Com, Diamond Multimedia, and the Sabre Network.

40.6 Notoriety

Versions of WinGate prior to 2.1d (1997) shipped with an insecure default configuration that - if not secured by the network administrator - allowed untrusted third parties to proxy network traffic through the WinGate server. This made open WinGate servers common targets of crackers looking for anonymous redirectors through which to attack other systems. While WinGate was by no means the only exploited proxy server, its wide popularity amongst users with little experience administering networks made it almost synonymous with open SOCKS proxies in the late 1990s.[2] Furthermore, since a restricted (2 users) version of the product was freely available without registration, contacting all WinGate users to notify of security issues was impossible, and therefore even long after the security problems were resolved there were still many insecure installations in use.

Some versions of the Sobig worm installed a pirated copy of WinGate 5 in a deliberately insecure configuration to be used by spammers. These installations used non-standard ports for SOCKS and WinGate remote control and so in general did not interfere with other software running on the infected host computer. This resulted in some antivirus software incorrectly identifying WinGate as malware and removing it.

40.7 WinGate 7

Development of WinGate 7 ran from early 2006 until its release in November 2011. Initially labelled WinGate 2007, a technical preview was eventually made available in June 2007, slated for release in early 2008. At this time, a new policy system was introduced, based around a flow-chart decision tree which provided complete user-control over policy structure. Soon after, this the product was re-labelled WinGate 2008. The year 2008 came and went without a WinGate release, as did 2009. Qbik, however, was still in full development of WinGate 7 (as it is now called) and moved their own company gateway to the product in December 2009.

From March 2010 betas of WinGate 7 were made available to people registered in the WinGate 7 beta program.

In September 2010 Qbik officially launched a YouTube channel showing a number of videos showing WinGate 7 in operation. The following month, Qbik opened up its WinGate 7 Beta forum to the general public.

On 28 May 2011 WinGate 7 entered public beta. Then, on 15 November 2011, the first official public releas of WinGate 7.0 (build 3332) was released.

40.8 Version history

40.9 See also

- Internet Security

40.10 References

[1] "WinGate 8 release notes". Retrieved 2014-10-28.

[2] "Exposing the Underground: Adventures of an Open Proxy Server". LURHQ. Retrieved 2007-02-04.

40.11 External links

- WinGate Proxy Server official site
- WinGate Proxy Server in Italy

Chapter 41

Zeroshell

Zeroshell is a small Linux distribution for servers and embedded systems which aims to provide network services. As its name implies, its administration relies on a web-based graphical interface. There is no need to use a shell to administer and configure it. Zeroshell is available as Live CD and CompactFlash images, and VMware virtual machines.

41.1 Selected features

- RADIUS server which is able to provide strong authentication for the Wireless clients by using IEEE 802.1X and Wi-Fi Protected Access (WPA/WPA2) protocols;

- Captive portal for network authentication in the HotSpots by using a web browser. The credentials can be verified against a Radius server, a Kerberos 5 KDC (such as Active Directory KDC);

- Netfilter – Firewall, Packet Filter and Stateful Packet Inspection (SPI), Layer 7 filter to block or shape the connections generated by Peer to Peer clients;

- Linux network scheduler – control maximum bandwidth, the guaranteed bandwidth and the priority of some types of traffic such as VoIP and peer-to-peer;

- VPN host-to-LAN and LAN-to-LAN with the IPSec/L2TP and OpenVPN protocols;

- Routing and Bridging capabilities with VLAN IEEE 802.1Q support;

- Multizone DNS (Domain name system) server;

- Multi subnet DHCP server;

- PPPoE client for connection to the WAN (Wide area network) via ADSL, DSL and cable lines;

- Dynamic DNS client updater for DynDNS;

- NTP (Network Time Protocol) client and server;

- Syslog server for receiving and cataloging the system logs produced by the remote hosts;

- Kerberos 5 authentication;

- LDAP server;

- X.509 certification authority.

41.2 Hardware

Zeroshell can be installed on any i386 architecture based computer with almost any Ethernet interface. It can also be installed on most embedded devices.

41.3 References

41.4 External links

- Zeroshell Website (English)

- Zeroshell Website (Italiano/Italian)

41.5 Text and image sources, contributors, and licenses

41.5.1 Text

- **Virtual private network** *Source:* https://en.wikipedia.org/wiki/Virtual_private_network?oldid=689643404 *Contributors:* CYD, Bryan Derksen, The Anome, Youssefsan, Aldie, Kurt Jansson, Heron, Nealmcb, Bewildebeast, David Martland, Hyakugei, Pnm, Kku, (, J'raxis, Glenn, Mxn, JidGom, Agaffin, Ww, Fuzheado, Phr, Wik, Chenghui~enwiki, Joshk, Bevo, Joy, Flockmeal, Carbuncle, PuzzletChung, Chuunen Baka, Robbot, Chealer, 1984, Nurg, Hadal, Jleedev, Tobias Bergemann, Yama, Inkling, Everyking, Fleminra, Gracefool, Matt Crypto, Jaan513, Alvestrand, Edcolins, Gadfium, Utcursch, Jackcsk, OverlordQ, Robert Brockway, Quarl, MFNickster, Godsmoke, Anirvan, Hellisp, Pascalv, EagleOne, Chrisbolt, Mike Rosoft, Seffer, Monkeyman, Discospinster, Rhobite, FT2, Izwalito~enwiki, YUL89YYZ, Bishopolis, ZeroOne, MattTM, JoeSmack, Evice, Dpotter, Pmcm, Szquirrel, Art LaPella, Gershwinrb, 2005, Bobo192, Ray Dassen, Robotje, Blonkm, John Vandenberg, Lkstrand, R. S. Shaw, Cwolfsheep, Pokrajac, Pearle, BlueNovember, ClementSeveillac, Paulehoffman, Jrapo, Alansohn, Gary, Anthony Appleyard, Andrewpmk, Andrew Gray, DreamGuy, Snowolf, GL, Nqtrung, RainbowOfLight, Tomlzz1, Pauli133, MeToo, Splurben, Nuno Tavares, Iceb, Woohookitty, Mindmatrix, RHaworth, LOL, Deeahbz, Unixer, Armando, Nklatt, Dmol, Torqueing, Marco-Tolo, Tslocum, RichardWeiss, Graham87, Niffweed17, Vanderdecken, Tlroche, Boardista, Rjwilmsi, Mkidson, Bruce1ee, Yamamoto Ichiro, Diablo-D3, FlaBot, Fijal, Sydbarrett74, Ground Zero, Ausinha, Winhunter, Aeon17x, RobyWayne, Intgr, David H Braun (1964), Mhking, Therefore, BlueJaeger, YurikBot, Wavelength, Borgx, Chris Mounce, Crazytales, Gardar Rurak, Mohsen Basirat, Stephenb, Manop, David Woodward, Kimchi.sg, Bovineone, Wimt, Thane, GSK, Długosz, Cleared as filed, Brandon, Jairo lopez, Bota47, Haemo, Xpclient, Wknight94, MCB, Zzuuzz, Closedmouth, Extraordinary, Abune, Drable, GraemeL, Vicarious, CWenger, Plyd, Rearden9, Whaa?, Snaxe920, Mebden, Eenu, Bswilson, Veinor, SmackBot, MattieTK, TheBilly, Mmernex, KnowledgeOfSelf, Ma8thew, C.Fred, AndreasJS, Delldot, Ieopo, BiT, SmartGuy Old, Gilliam, Skizzik, Angelbo, Talinus, BirdValiant, Amux, BenAveling, Maxgrin, Chris the speller, Apankrat, Thumperward, Oli Filth, EncMstr, MalafayaBot, RayAYang, Deli nk, Jerome Charles Potts, Octahedron80, DHN-bot~enwiki, Invenio, Gracenotes, JGXenite, Chuckw, Tsca.bot, Can't sleep, clown will eat me, ThePromenader, Tryggvia, RFightmaster, JonHarder, ElTopo~enwiki, RedHillian, Krich, Ianmacm, Decltype, WarrenA, Trailbum, Springnuts, DKEdwards, Ohconfucius, Lexicontra, Kuru, Mr.Clown, Minna Sora no Shita, Lucaweb, Chrisch, JHunterJ, Noah Salzman, Jadams76, Swartik, Brainix, Fangfufu, TastyPoutine, Negrulio, Kvng, Informedbanker, HisSpaceResearch, Peter M Dodge, Michael Shade, Jfayel, Az1568, Deice, Tawkerbot2, Kielvon, Ashwin ambekar, CmdrObot, PuerExMachina, PorthosBot, Alexamies, Funnyfarmofdoom, Phatom87, Rocketron5, W.F.Galway, Ntsimp, Djg2006, Michaelas10, Corpx, Shandon, AlexeyN, Chupacabras, Jrgetsin, M. B., Jr., Optimist on the run, Scarpy, Omicronpersei8, Thijs!bot, Epbr123, IvanStepaniuk, Tahren B, Hcberkowitz, John254, Cr0w, E. Ripley, Kaaveh Ahangar~enwiki, CharlotteWebb, Natalie Erin, Escarbot, Rees11, Davidoff, Ministry of Truth, Majorly, Saimhe, Luna Santin, Widefox, Dbrodbeck, Isilanes, Mercury543210, Eubene, Res2216firestar, Harryzilber, RM MARTIN, Barek, MER-C, LeedsKing, Sintesia, Gaurav.khatri, Raanoo, Drugonot, Magioladitis, VoABot II, Sijokjose, Alphawave, JNW, JamesBWatson, Froid, Foxb, Elinruby, Allstarecho, DerHexer, Tom Foley, Ben 9876, Jonomacdrones, MartinBot, Webster21, Ironman5247, Jim.henderson, R'n'B, Kateshortforbob, Pekaje, Jmccormac, Me.rs, Wodkreso, J.delanoy, Trusilver, Reliablehosting, Thaurisil, Wiki 101, Skier Dude, TehPhil, WebHamster, AntiSpamBot, Robigus, BrianOfRugby, Jazappi, FJPB, Juliancolton, Cometstyles, Redlazer, Pdcook, Ja 62, Zeroshell, Philomathoholic, VolkovBot, Nardixsempre, Jcap1ln, Chris400, Schecky4, Philip Trueman, DoorsAjar, Neoalian, Khag7, TonyUK, Rgore, Leafyplant, Broadbot, Jackfork, LeaveSleaves, Bbbone, ARTamb, Belmontian, Smithkkj, Falcon8765, YordanGeorgiev, LittleBenW, Finnrind, Kbrose, SieBot, Nubiatech, Azadk, SilentAshes, Prakash Nadkarni, Americaninseoul, Vjardin, Winchelsea, Gerakibot, Mashouri, Shijiree88, Novastorm, Happysailor, Rninneman, Jojalozzo, FAchi, Avaarga, CutOffTies, Cfleisch, Doctorfluffy, Sgarson, Netmotion1234, Nuttycoconut, Lightmouse, LindArlaud, Torchwoodwho, Huggi, Foggy Morning, Ken123BOT, Brwave, Escape Orbit, ShelleyAdams, Tuxa, WakingLili, Elassint, ClueBot, Vladkornea, Hal 2001, Wikievil666, The Thing That Should Not Be, EoGuy, Rich45, Plat'Home, Tomlee1968, Jdzarlino, Excirial, Alexbot, Anon lynx, PixelBot, Blacklogic, Vanisheduser12345, TheRedPenOfDoom, Razorflame, SecurityManager, Ottawa4ever, Eli77e, WEJohnston, Pinchomic, Johnuniq, SoxBot III, LetMeLookItUp, Ginbot86, Lmstearn, XLinkBot, Aaron north, Smartchain, Dthomsen8, Skarebo, Fosterbt, Dgtsyb, MystBot, Williameboley, Thatguyflint, Addbot, Nacnud22032, TheNeutroniumAlchemist, Fieldday-sunday, MagnusA.Bot, MrOllie, Dmktg, Glane23, SamatBot, Jasper Deng, Тиверополник, Tide rolls, Lightbot, SPat, Legobot, Luckas-bot, Yobot, Ptbotgourou, Dugnad, Les boys, Kikbguy, THEN WHO WAS PHONE?, Nallimbot, AnomieBOT, DemocraticLuntz, Floquenbeam, Rubinbot, Jlavepoze, Efa, Jim1138, Gascreed, Aditya, Materialscientist, Danno uk, ArthurBot, DirlBot, Xqbot, Apothecia, DrFausty, Fancy steve, Jmundo, Karlzt, PositiveNetworks, GrouchoBot, Webwat, Kevinzhouyan, SassoBot, GenOrl, Visiting1, Brandoas, Smallman12q, Shadowjams, 33rogers, A.amitkumar, Prari, FrescoBot, Selah28, Mu Mind, Ozhu, VS6507, Peteinterpol, Tech editor007, Emmatheartist, Winterst, Pinethicket, I dream of horses, Edderso, Ziabhat, MastiBot, Gkstyle, Serols, SpaceFlight89, Jandalhandler, Movingonup, Sunny2who, ShorelineWA, Tim1357, Timurx, Mjs1991, Mercy11, Stdundon, Azerrima, Adi4094, TheMesquito, K-secure, Tuxcrafter~enwiki, Onel5969, Mean as custard, RjwilmsiBot, Ripchip Bot, Regancy42, START-newsgroup, EmausBot, Dewritech, Vickey2020, Enqueror, EleferenBot, Solarra, Braviojk, Tommy2010, Wikipelli, AsceticRose, Wackywace, Ludovic.ferre, JamesGeddes, Jino123, Superpixelpro, Katkay, Kilopi, Barekpublic, Scott.somohano, L Kensington, Daiyuu, MainFrame, Humannetwork, Sepersann, JaredThornbridge, ClueBot NG, Rafigordon, Satellizer, Evansda, Rosothefox, Sajjad36122061, Widr, Bigjust12345, Katkay1, Nobletripe, Naba san, Strike Eagle, DBigXray, BG19bot, Bmusician, Wikingtubby, Jeremiah.l.burns, Sujathasubhash, Acole67, Ywalker79, Irulet, Snow Blizzard, Sleepsfortheweak, Akapribot, Teknetz, Miabchdave, Nkansahrexford, Pratyya Ghosh, ProfPolySci45, EuroCarGT, Raprap321, Mfalaura, Cligra, Student geek, Cpartsenidis, Jags707, Corinna128, Shierro, Pete Mahen, TwoTwoHello, TechyOne, Lugia2453, Frosty, Jemappelleungarcon, Jamesx12345, Gurdipsclick, Epater, Jamesmcmahon0, VPN.PRO, AnthonyJ Lock, Maura Driscoll, DavidLeighEllis, R00stare, AlewisGB, Haminoon, Kamesg, Xenomm, Rashoba, Burroomens3, Slunkbroil, Jwp9023, TheDailyFlows, Akhilufp, Vieque, Trueinternetworld, Openrouter, ITouchHacker, Amortias, PhiladelphiaInjustice, Marthastacey, Kdenery, Walt3rste1nbucher, Sturtr, Letrus~enwiki, Charlie9861, ToonLucas22, Cajidali27, Joseph2302, Harbo5, Inivanoff1, Erik.moorefield, Debiannut, Anarchyte, Afaflakjn, ProprioMe OW, The Quixotic Potato, Rukhsana Fareed, JamesVang86, Kurousagi, Andrewjackson1029, Tcpvpn, Sandip760, Amyacker, VeVeMe, Tgva, Shaheen27, Zju hac, Zeeshanmrit and Anonymous: 1174

- **AceVPN** *Source:* https://en.wikipedia.org/wiki/AceVPN?oldid=678786554 *Contributors:* Savonneux, DaltonCastle, Vansockslayer and Anonymous: 1

- **AnchorFree** *Source:* https://en.wikipedia.org/wiki/AnchorFree?oldid=686241672 *Contributors:* Rwalker, Microchip08, EdJohnston, Widefox, DGG, Yintan, Yobot, Ulric1313, GoingBatty, Stringybark, Senator2029, BG19bot, BattyBot, CitizenNeutral, Rybec, Rdoates, Randomalando, Split25 and Anonymous: 11

- **Avast! SecureLine VPN** *Source:* https://en.wikipedia.org/wiki/Avast!_SecureLine_VPN?oldid=670644490 *Contributors:* Bearcat, SJ Defender and Anarchyte

- **BTGuard** *Source:* https://en.wikipedia.org/wiki/BTGuard?oldid=640733070 *Contributors:* Yobot, Everymorning, Goalbox, SuperHeroTurtle and Anonymous: 2

- **CAPRI OS** *Source:* https://en.wikipedia.org/wiki/CAPRI_OS?oldid=688922124 *Contributors:* Philipwhiuk, Niceguyedc, Boomur, Yobot, Santryl, TheJJJunk and Fixuture

- **Darknet** *Source:* https://en.wikipedia.org/wiki/Darknet?oldid=688471751 *Contributors:* M~enwiki, Shii, Lousyd, Delirium, CesarB, Haakon, DropDeadGorgias, Ciphergoth, Scott, Thomas~enwiki, Vodex, TJ, K1Bond007, Dbabbitt, MilkMiruku, DocWatson42, Obli, Neuro, Terrible Tim, Stuuf, AlistairMcMillan, RadioYeti, Chaikney, Kusunose, Creidieki, Usrnme h8er, Alkivar, LindsayH, Cmdrjameson, Blenda~enwiki, Ziggurat, Giraffedata, Scubacuda, Wtmitchell, Markaci, Alvis, Vorash, Eyreland, Qwertyus, GrundyCamellia, Phillipedison1891, XP1, RobertG, Last1in, JYOuyang, Eldred, Wongm, Intgr, Benlisquare, Dadu~enwiki, Thodin, Remmelt, Jimp, Hydrargyrum, Romanc19s, Irishguy, Deku-shrub, GeoffCapp, Ninly, MarkTAW, RamirBorja, Jonasfagundes, Finell, Arasb~enwiki, That Guy, From That Show!, Iancjclarke, MacsBug, SmackBot, MeiStone, Cassivs, A. B., Shadow7789, Frap, JonHarder, Marc-André Aßbrock, Michael Rogers, Writtenonsand, CoolKoon, 16@r, Anonymous anonymous, Norm mit, Twas Now, Pbaehr, Tawkerbot2, JebJoya, PuerExMachina, Cydebot, DumbBOT, Biblbroks, Rapidconfusion, East718, AshishKulkarni, Litening, Ginoslug, WLU, Wkussmaul, ExplicitImplicity, RockMFR, Rovingardener, Maurice Carbonaro, Touisiau, AntiSpamBot, Rei-bot, Econterms, THC Loadee, Jsysinc, Sempcom, Joydeep jra, ClueBot, Fyyer, Cambrasa, Sv1xv, Excirial, Rhododendrites, Arjayay, Badfoo, Baudway, LeheckaG, Addbot, Ztnorman, Favonian, Lightbot, SasiSasi, Yobot, Amirobot, AnomieBOT, Materialscientist, Alumnum, FrescoBot, CSEMike, Desnacked, LittleWink, Pmokeefe, Pdreiss, RjwilmsiBot, Pegaze34, Dewritech, Ewhunter, Wingman4l7, LWG, ChuispastonBot, LZ6387, Wluce0, ClueBot NG, Jaobar, Vincent Moon, ProcMoss, Csoler, Helpful Pixie Bot, Emisanle, BG19bot, AgentEm84, The Almightey Drill, Ĉiuĵaŭde, BattyBot, DarafshBot, Fragga, Rogikalomni, Nodove, Kahtar, Fixuture, Monkbot, Lymaniffy, Jtronn, FoordH and Anonymous: 134

- **Decentralized network 42** *Source:* https://en.wikipedia.org/wiki/Decentralized_network_42?oldid=674748988 *Contributors:* Rpyle731, Woohookitty, Jimp, RussBot, Bhny, Xuu, Deku-shrub, Chris the speller, Frap, Prunk, Widefox, Olipro, Rhododendrites, Life of Riley, Yobot, Materialscientist, LilHelpa, FrescoBot, Teapeat, BG19bot, Zorun, Eeadc, Fgegypt, NixNodes and Anonymous: 5

- **DirectAccess** *Source:* https://en.wikipedia.org/wiki/DirectAccess?oldid=674672235 *Contributors:* The Anome, Phil Boswell, Rchandra, ConradPino, YUL89YYZ, Cwolfsheep, Rjwilmsi, Voidxor, SmackBot, Chris the speller, Frap, Stonesand, Cydebot, Hebrides, John Ericson, Gohan71, Addbot, Buster7, Debresser, Jasper Deng, Luckas-bot, Bunnyhop11, AnomieBOT, Rubinbot, LilHelpa, Kevinzhouyan, Winterst, JosephDavies, Thexchair, Scott.somohano, MainFrame, BenAriAtMicrosoft, Hz.tiang, Rpavlik, Richardhicks00, Ugog Nizdast, Raydev1, AgileHumor, Ender2126, DuesHex and Anonymous: 43

- **Dynamic Multipoint Virtual Private Network** *Source:* https://en.wikipedia.org/wiki/Dynamic_Multipoint_Virtual_Private_Network?oldid=688353765 *Contributors:* Cwolfsheep, Giraffedata, Rajah, Kenyon, Woohookitty, MarcoTolo, Groink, SmackBot, Snori, Sadads, Datashark, BryanG, A5b, Jbrunner007, Mblumber, MarshBot, AntiVandalBot, Xhienne, Epeefleche, Kaitwospirit, Bissinger, R'n'B, Funandtrvl, Dstary, Kbrose, Addbot, Pipemartinm, Yobot, 521gcm, Xqbot, Skyerise, Bomazi, Evansda, Sowsnek, Audiofreak21, BattyBot, M.sullenberger, Yetanotheracct, Spumuq and Anonymous: 26

- **FreeLAN** *Source:* https://en.wikipedia.org/wiki/FreeLAN?oldid=684863458 *Contributors:* Bgwhite, Dialectric, AnomieBOT, Redrose64, Mean as custard, BG19bot, OccultZone, Brunobeaufils, Unician, Richman1000000 and Anonymous: 3

- **LogMeIn Hamachi** *Source:* https://en.wikipedia.org/wiki/LogMeIn_Hamachi?oldid=678890676 *Contributors:* Haakon, Glenn, Ehn, Fuzheado, Omegatron, Bevo, Lowellian, Jae, Lproven, Gilgamesh~enwiki, Gracefool, AlistairMcMillan, Kusunose, Am088, Ilgiz, Imjustmatthew, Maikel, Slady, Discospinster, Plugwash, CanisRufus, Afed, Bobo192, Cwolfsheep, Foobaz, Guspaz, GNU4eva, CyberSkull, Jeltz, Fritz Saalfeld, Sligocki, Hu, Falcorian, Christian *Yendi* Severin, LOL, SergeyLitvinov, Maros, Karlww, Josh Parris, JMCorey, Nneonneo, MapsMan, FlaBot, Spaceman85, Stoph, Nihiltres, RexNL, Melancholie, Alvin-cs, Sherool, SirGrant, Mpontes, Jengelh, CambridgeBayWeather, Ugur Basak, Sir48, SixSix, Hugo 87, Mütze, TheSeer, Sandstein, Riptor3000, Chase me ladies, I'm the Cavalry, GraemeL, Flood of SYNs, Tenox, Fsiler, Jade Knight, DFulbright, Matt Heard, Veinor, BonsaiViking, SmackBot, Verdafolio, Ccscott, Gilliam, Fogster, Centralkong, Apankrat, BarkerJr, Snori, King Arthur6687, Silent SAM, DHN-bot~enwiki, LeiZhu, Frap, AlternativePlus, ElTopo~enwiki, Addshore, Acdx, TJJFV, Xlaran, Joffeloff, BioTube, Beetstra, Djlarz, Jason.grossman, George100, Altonbr, SkyWalker, JForget, Synthmon, Nczempin, Random name, NTDOY Fanboy, Tim1988, Cydebot, Thijs!bot, Unicyclopedia, Vmadeira, A3RO, Tarnavski, Ericjs, Mentifisto, Rees11, Ministry of Truth, Gioto, Widefox, Gilson.soares, 3R1C, Dreaded Walrus, JAnDbot, Leuko, Aka042, Tins128, DerHexer, FlieGerFaUstMe262, CommonsDelinker, Trusilver, Jofafrazze, ZinnKid, Themathkid, Remember the dot, Neocodesoftware, KGV, BBilge, Somejan, Lexein, Mars93, PNG crusade bot, Nihad Hamzic~enwiki, A4bot, Rogerdpack, Georgewblack, Sparrowman980, Nition1, Happysailor, Antonio Lopez, Crisis, Haris.tv, Denisarona, SiL!, Emk, Slaporte, Elassint, ClueBot, PipepBot, Tobenvontoben, Plat'Home, Mosn1, Eirlys001, Failure.exe, Paul-lmi, Muro Bot, El bot de la dieta, KevinMalachowski, Dank, Wdustbuster, Expertjohn, XLinkBot, WikHead, Salam32, IsmaelLuceno, Addbot, AJPOD, Yousou, SpBot, Jasper Deng, Tide rolls, Matěj Grabovský, The Bushranger, Luckas-bot, Yobot, Fraggle81, Kikbguy, KamikazeBot, AnomieBOT, IRP, Pijusmagnificus82~enwiki, Ipatrol, Renatofig, Avesus, Lkt1126, ZajDee, Obersachsebot, GrouchoBot, Kevinzhouyan, Cybjit, Shadowjams, Csgerg, FrescoBot, HJ Mitchell, Xhaoz, Anderhil, Edderso, Nikkolla, Banej, Azdergeri, Ribulose, Lopifalko, DASHBot, EmausBot, Racerx11, Hungryman12, Wowxiaojj, ZéroBot, Bollyjeff, Asmerok, SweetFlavor, Tomy9510, Coasterlover1994, AnonymousPenguin10, Kris159, ClueBot NG, AlbertBickford, Matthiaspaul, Jenova20, Thedemon007, Patrias, IAmTheCandyman, Bs27975, Leochiffriller, Linux731, 13375up4h4x0r, TiloWiki, DuoDex, Webclient101, Dumanyack, WikiTyson, LOLchicken, GreatMarkO, Pyscowicz, InAUGral, Knismogenic, ScotXW, Patrios, Vieque, Owleaf, Ericrct, ZerockGNU and Anonymous: 371

- **Hola (VPN)** *Source:* https://en.wikipedia.org/wiki/Hola_(VPN)?oldid=685143199 *Contributors:* Alexf, Jhertel, Jesse Viviano, Bentogoa, Niceguyedc, Dthomsen8, Yobot, AnomieBOT, Jandalhandler, Onel5969, Gareth Griffith-Jones, Loriendrew, Davidbfranks, Lucky102, AnnaPaw, Delhiidevils, Aliblogger1985, Nina87white, Entertainment Seven Twenty, Ng49 and Anonymous: 17

- **Hotspot Shield** *Source:* https://en.wikipedia.org/wiki/Hotspot_Shield?oldid=687859023 *Contributors:* Bearcat, Goudzovski, Bgwhite, C.Fred, Doctorhawkes, NatGertler, Wylve, KylieTastic, Macdonald-ross, Djmips, Niceguyedc, Yobot, AnomieBOT, Materialscientist, RjwilmsiBot, EmausBot, ClueBot NG, Widr, BG19bot, Frosty, Epicgenius, Tiszteletem!, Thearighter, Spacejammer, Dubsted ted, Porcelian cragi, Thegreat34, Wickedsoxfan34, PhiladelphiaInjustice, Euro-maidan-begening, Esquivalience, Vobzkie and Anonymous: 28

- **Ipredator** *Source:* https://en.wikipedia.org/wiki/Ipredator?oldid=673640164 *Contributors:* Damian Yerrick, Kjetil r, Piotrus, Quirk, Billy-mac00, VBGFscJUn3, Sedimin, Woohookitty, Dananderson, Rjwilmsi, RussBot, Keithonearth, Fergofrog, KiloByte, Kanji~enwiki, Robofish, Cydebot, Jojan, JustAGal, JAnDbot, Maskiner, Roberth Edberg, Connor Behan, Happysailor, John Nevard, SF007, Addbot, Yobot, 33rogers, LucienBOT, 4bpp, Thomas von der Lippe, Jesus Presley, EmausBot, Tuankiet65, Chorkman, K kisses, Sparthorse, Bpoojary, ThisIsAlanB and Anonymous: 41

- **KAME project** *Source:* https://en.wikipedia.org/wiki/KAME_project?oldid=664869347 *Contributors:* Egil, Fudoreaper, Ezhar Fairlight, Rich Farmbrough, Orlady, Ghen, Janizary, SmackBot, AJG, Eskimbot, Frap, Magioladitis, Gwern, Sesshomaru, Charliel 94, Int21h, Addbot, Xqbot, Winterst, Wondigoma, Bkouhi, Dcvmoole and Anonymous: 16

- **Kerio Control** *Source:* https://en.wikipedia.org/wiki/Kerio_Control?oldid=686794731 *Contributors:* Golem~enwiki, Ihcoyc, Andrewman327, Rebroad, Umapathy, Tangotango, Ucucha, Tedder, Hm2k, SmackBot, Timotheus Canens, Thumperward, OrphanBot, Ihatetoregister, Fast.ch, Fernvale, DanielRigal, Anthony Bradbury, Cydebot, BetacommandBot, Kjwu, Stephenchou0722, ImageRemovalBot, DavidGGG, Addbot, Vyom25, Luckas-bot, Rubinbot, SassoBot, Full-date unlinking bot, FoxBot, Dewritech, Wbm1058, TheKarpati, Codename Lisa, Carstenmaas, Mahafuzur 13, Coco Espinosa and Anonymous: 16

- **Layer 2 Tunneling Protocol** *Source:* https://en.wikipedia.org/wiki/Layer_2_Tunneling_Protocol?oldid=689166193 *Contributors:* AxelBoldt, The Anome, Nate Silva, Edward, Yaronf, Saltine, MrJones, Chealer, Frencheigh, Ferdinand Pienaar, JTN, IlyaHaykinson, Dmeranda, Srbauer, Spearhead, Sietse Snel, Aaronbrick, Cwolfsheep, Apyule, Wrs1864, Ynhockey, Stephan Leeds, K3rb, Voxadam, Ylem, John Cardinal, ^demon, Mendaliv, Oblivious, FlaBot, TheAnarcat, CiaPan, Moocha, Borgx, Cryptic, Muruga86, NawlinWiki, CecilWard, Zwobot, Xpclient, Smack-Bot, Unyoyega, Eskimbot, Ohnoitsjamie, Daedalus01, Nealc, Walkerhamilton, Matieux, MureninC, A5b, Cibu, JHunterJ, Infofarmer, Peyre, Tawkerbot2, CmdrObot, Cydebot, Mato, Gogo Dodo, Thijs!bot, Epbr123, Enjoi4586, Web-Crawling Stickler, NescioNomen, Hom sepanta, Free49498445, Andareed, Dispenser, Metaclassing, Mdmkolbe, NPrice, Rednectar.chris, Kbrose, SieBot, Vjardin, Mwaisberg, Plat'Home, Anon lynx, Muhandes, SilvonenBot, Addbot, MrOllie, Luckas-bot, AnomieBOT, Materialscientist, Shadowjams, Some standardized rigour, Mmtmmt, W Nowicki, Skeffling, DrilBot, LittleWink, Jandalhandler, Ripchip Bot, EmausBot, WikitanvirBot, ZéroBot, Fontoponto, ClueBot NG, Wbm1058, ChrisGualtieri, Xauen~enwiki, TechyOne, Captain Conundrum, Krankes-kind, ArmbrustBot, Jerimiah McCain, I.moskalev, AmazingHulk and Anonymous: 109

- **Libreswan** *Source:* https://en.wikipedia.org/wiki/Libreswan?oldid=687722313 *Contributors:* Pigsonthewing, Atomsmith, Txt.file, Josve05a, ChrisGualtieri, Dcclayton and Anonymous: 5

- **N2n** *Source:* https://en.wikipedia.org/wiki/N2n?oldid=644437672 *Contributors:* Tange, Alaric, Rich Farmbrough, Cwolfsheep, Amontero, Justin Ormont, Overand, DTOx, JLaTondre, SmackBot, Od Mishehu, Frap, MonsieurET, Wkussmaul, Gu1dry, Muhandes, Addbot, AlexandrDmitri, Yobot, Amirobot, LittleWink, Aavindraa, AzertyFab, Rancher 42, IluvatarBot and Anonymous: 18

- **Network Extrusion** *Source:* https://en.wikipedia.org/wiki/Network_Extrusion?oldid=589944153 *Contributors:* Bearcat, Mcr314, Mandarax, Katharineamy, Jasper Deng, LilHelpa and Anonymous: 1

- **OpenConnect** *Source:* https://en.wikipedia.org/wiki/OpenConnect?oldid=659819077 *Contributors:* Frap, Nmav, Yobot, Winterst, Jandalhandler, Txt.file and Anonymous: 7

- **Openswan** *Source:* https://en.wikipedia.org/wiki/Openswan?oldid=683208683 *Contributors:* Edward, KAMiKAZOW, Joy, Sn0wflake, Katherine Shaw, Cwolfsheep, Mcr314, Mr flea, Wisq, Sleepyhead81, Isuldor, SmackBot, Pioto, Frap, Isilanes, Speck-Made, CommonsDelinker, Arite, Nimhs, EmxBot, Uzytkownik, Kl4m-AWB, Plat'Home, Addbot, Mabdul, Jandalhandler, Txt.file, Xmteam, AXRL, Etrillaud, Aavindraa, BG19bot, Tianjiao, Toxiczka, J744, Dcclayton and Anonymous: 21

- **OpenVPN** *Source:* https://en.wikipedia.org/wiki/OpenVPN?oldid=681697507 *Contributors:* Bryan Derksen, Pagingmrherman, ZoeB, Glenn, Jonik, Ehn, Disdero, Bevo, LX, Inter, Karn, Fleminra, AlistairMcMillan, Matt Crypto, PlatinumX, Dfwiki, SURIV, Elektron, Smokris, Archer3, Pmsyyz, Bender235, Shanes, Sietse Snel, Cwolfsheep, Apyule, RoySmith, Schapel, Mr700, Stephan Leeds, Poppafuze, Karnesky, Mindmatrix, Crucis, Justin Ormont, Bensin, FlaBot, Daderot, Ghen, Intgr, Mattman00000, Alvin-cs, Ahunt, Jamesyonan, YurikBot, LiX, Family Guy Guy, KyjL, MMuzammils, Shaddack, Leotohill, GraemeL, SmackBot, TheBilly, Wlindley, Binarypower, Carpetsmoker, Thumperward, EncMstr, PersistentLurker, Deli nk, DHN-bot~enwiki, Jdthood, Ivankb, Frap, JonHarder, Jmnbatista, Albertalbs, Guyjohnston, Nmav, Antonielly, Larrymcp, Fmusinguzi, Dautranhsinhton, TiagoPereira, Webash, Phatom87, AndrewHowse, Teratornis, Scarpy, JamesAM, Neil916, Boris Friedrichs~enwiki, Seaphoto, MaTT~enwiki, Isilanes, JAnDbot, NapoliRoma, Barek, Magioladitis, Marycontrary, CommonsDelinker, Robertducon, Idioma-bot, Lexein, Ggeller, TXiKiBoT, Alonbl, Rjgodoy, Enviroboy, Kbrose, Coj, Nubiatech, VVVBot, Wilhelmina clemenso, Cintema, Rafesq, Autumn Wind, HighInBC, Joseluisfb, Ecrist, Plat'Home, Niceguyedc, PixelBot, Garing, XLinkBot, Alanthehat, Addbot, Innv, MrOllie, Jasper Deng, Mlpotgieter, Zorrobot, Luckas-bot, Yobot, Kikbguy, Götz, Efa, Xqbot, PabloCastellano, Klisanor, Kevinzhouyan, Cvandeplas, GutoCarvalho, FrescoBot, Hexafluoride, Smeago, Alainamedeus, Boobarkee, Andreystrelkov, FoxBot, Wzyboy, Plaisthos, EugeneKay, Ripchip Bot, Lopifalko, Imcon, Dewritech, Aavindraa, GuizmOVPN, Sbmeirow, Daiyuu, Karthik.upadhyayula, ClueBot NG, Jbekkema, Sabroadley, Delusion23, Cntras, Thelle, SameOff, BG19bot, Wikingtubby, Christophocles, Hz.tiang, Rancher 42, Irulet, Kristian.luck, Chris-Gualtieri, Dexbot, Xauen~enwiki, Tsepty, MartinMichlmayr, AndyLim091, SolarStarSpire, Deedsnance, Epater, Jodosma, Pokechu22, Theklun, Rashob, Rashoba, Tobmaster1985, Mrmattu, Paulinemoore111, کامل‌الدار, TheHoster, Reviewstime, Fipevpn, Proxysp, Inivanoff1, Supdiop, Packt Publishing and Anonymous: 193

- **Private Internet Access** *Source:* https://en.wikipedia.org/wiki/Private_Internet_Access?oldid=685625486 *Contributors:* Rwalker, Twsx, Throop, Graham king 3, Americanfreedom, Yobot, SL93, C4K3, Mean as custard, ClueBot NG, Masssly, Realrasengan, Samwalton9, Shaunstevin, Fixuture, TheCoffeeAddict, Cyanhat, Bleuhat, TristenlottNJP, Aliahmed314, Bartmoor, Peterjosling, BasketOfShrimp, Explode2011 and Anonymous: 4

- **Social VPN** *Source:* https://en.wikipedia.org/wiki/Social_VPN?oldid=669368080 *Contributors:* Haakon, Behnam, MBisanz, Cwolfsheep, Mdd, Amalthea, SmackBot, Frap, Abi79, CmdrObot, Scarpy, Jojalozzo, JL-Bot, MuZemike, AnomieBOT, Ptony82, Renatofig, Kevinzhouyan, John of Reading, Aavindraa, Gummismari, Lesser Cartographies, Jackmcbarn, Saectar and Anonymous: 11

- **SoftEther Corporation** *Source:* https://en.wikipedia.org/wiki/SoftEther_Corporation?oldid=623510519 *Contributors:* Phr, Kusunose, RadioActive~enwiki, YurikBot, Kimchi.sg, Dialectric, Retired username, Od Mishehu, Xaosflux, Bluebot, Fangfufu, Cydebot, ForbiddenWord, Emesee, Martarius, Plat'Home, Sun Creator, Addbot, AnomieBOT, DrilBot, Daiyuu, Naba san, Y717 and Anonymous: 5

41.5.2 Images

- **File:Simple_Threenix_Installation_Block_Diagram.png** *Source:* https://upload.wikimedia.org/wikipedia/commons/2/25/Simple_Threenix_ Installation_Block_Diagram.png *License:* CC BY-SA 3.0 *Contributors:* Own work *Original artist:* Luca.gammelli

- **File:Softethervpn_fdb.jpg** *Source:* https://upload.wikimedia.org/wikipedia/commons/5/52/Softethervpn_fdb.jpg *License:* CC BY-SA 3.0 *Contributors:* Own work *Original artist:* Daiyuu

- **File:Softethervpn_ipsec.jpg** *Source:* https://upload.wikimedia.org/wikipedia/commons/f/f2/Softethervpn_ipsec.jpg *License:* CC BY-SA 3.0 *Contributors:* Own work *Original artist:* Daiyuu

- **File:Softethervpn_logo.jpg** *Source:* https://upload.wikimedia.org/wikipedia/commons/f/ff/Softethervpn_logo.jpg *License:* CC BY-SA 3.0 *Contributors:* Own work *Original artist:* Daiyuu

- **File:Softethervpn_ss.jpg** *Source:* https://upload.wikimedia.org/wikipedia/commons/e/e8/Softethervpn_ss.jpg *License:* CC BY-SA 3.0 *Contributors:* Own work *Original artist:* Daiyuu

- **File:Softethervpn_stack.jpg** *Source:* https://upload.wikimedia.org/wikipedia/commons/b/b2/Softethervpn_stack.jpg *License:* CC BY-SA 3.0 *Contributors:* Own work *Original artist:* Daiyuu

- **File:Softethervpn_trans.jpg** *Source:* https://upload.wikimedia.org/wikipedia/commons/5/59/Softethervpn_trans.jpg *License:* CC BY-SA 3.0 *Contributors:* Own work *Original artist:* Daiyuu

- **File:StrongSwan_UML_topology.png** *Source:* https://upload.wikimedia.org/wikipedia/en/7/78/StrongSwan_UML_topology.png *License:* Cc-by-sa-3.0 *Contributors:* ? *Original artist:* ?

- **File:Stylized_eye.svg** *Source:* https://upload.wikimedia.org/wikipedia/commons/4/4c/Stylized_eye.svg *License:* CC0 *Contributors:* Own work *Original artist:* camelNotation

- **File:Symbol_list_class.svg** *Source:* https://upload.wikimedia.org/wikipedia/en/d/db/Symbol_list_class.svg *License:* Public domain *Contributors:* ? *Original artist:* ?

- **File:Symbol_neutral_vote.svg** *Source:* https://upload.wikimedia.org/wikipedia/en/8/89/Symbol_neutral_vote.svg *License:* Public domain *Contributors:* ? *Original artist:* ?

- **File:System-installer.svg** *Source:* https://upload.wikimedia.org/wikipedia/commons/d/db/System-installer.svg *License:* Public domain *Contributors:* The Tango! Desktop Project *Original artist:* The people from the Tango! project

- **File:Threenix_logo_PNG.png** *Source:* https://upload.wikimedia.org/wikipedia/commons/d/d4/Threenix_logo_PNG.png *License:* CC BY-SA 3.0 *Contributors:* Own work *Original artist:* Luca.gammelli

- **File:Tor-logo-2011-flat.svg** *Source:* https://upload.wikimedia.org/wikipedia/commons/1/15/Tor-logo-2011-flat.svg *License:* CC BY 3.0 *Contributors:* https://media.torproject.org/image/official-images/2011-tor-logo-flat.svg *Original artist:* Tor Project

- **File:TunnelBear_Connected_USA.jpg** *Source:* https://upload.wikimedia.org/wikipedia/en/b/b7/TunnelBear_Connected_USA.jpg *License:* Fair use *Contributors:* Screenshot taken by uploader, User:Anarchyte *Original artist:* TunnelBear Inc

- **File:TunnelBear_Logo.png** *Source:* https://upload.wikimedia.org/wikipedia/en/c/c5/TunnelBear_Logo.png *License:* Fair use *Contributors:* https://www.tunnelbear.com/ *Original artist:* ?

- **File:TunnelBear_popup.jpg** *Source:* https://upload.wikimedia.org/wikipedia/en/6/6f/TunnelBear_popup.jpg *License:* Fair use *Contributors:* Screenshot taken by the uploader, User:Anarchyte *Original artist:* TunnelBear Inc

- **File:US-GreatSeal-Obverse.svg** *Source:* https://upload.wikimedia.org/wikipedia/commons/5/5c/Great_Seal_of_the_United_States_%28obverse% 29.svg *License:* Public domain *Contributors:* Extracted from PDF version of *Our Flag*, available here (direct PDF URL here.) *Original artist:* U.S. Government

- **File:Unbalanced_scales.svg** *Source:* https://upload.wikimedia.org/wikipedia/commons/f/fe/Unbalanced_scales.svg *License:* Public domain *Contributors:* ? *Original artist:* ?

- **File:VNS3_Manager_Status_Page.png** *Source:* https://upload.wikimedia.org/wikipedia/commons/1/13/VNS3_Manager_Status_Page.png *License:* CC BY-SA 3.0 *Contributors:* Own work *Original artist:* ObruniYaa

- **File:Virtual_Private_Network_overview.svg** *Source:* https://upload.wikimedia.org/wikipedia/commons/0/00/Virtual_Private_Network_overview. svg *License:* GFDL *Contributors:* Own work *Original artist:* Ludovic.ferre (talk · contribs)

- **File:VyOS.png** *Source:* https://upload.wikimedia.org/wikipedia/commons/4/4e/VyOS.png *License:* GFDL 1.3 *Contributors:* http://vyos.net *Original artist:* VyOS

- **File:Vyatta_trans_200.png** *Source:* https://upload.wikimedia.org/wikipedia/en/7/72/Vyatta_trans_200.png *License:* Fair use *Contributors:* The logo is from the http://www.vyatta.com website. *Original artist:* ?

- **File:Wiki_letter_w.svg** *Source:* https://upload.wikimedia.org/wikipedia/en/6/6c/Wiki_letter_w.svg *License:* Cc-by-sa-3.0 *Contributors:* ? *Original artist:* ?

41.5.3 Content license

- Creative Commons Attribution-Share Alike 3.0